Zen Meditation

Zen Meditation
A Broad View

by Justin F. Stone

GOOD KARMA
Fort Yates
1995

GOOD KARMA PUBLISHING, Inc., Publisher
P.O. Box 511 - 202 Main Street
Fort Yates, ND 58538

Printed in the United States of America

First Good Karma Publishing, Inc. edition - 1995
Second Printing - 1998

Cover photo - Hui-neng, Sixth Patriarch
Cover photo inset & photos on pp. 21, 23 - Jim Burns
Photos from personal collection of Justin F. Stone

Design & layout by Jean Katus

Text printed on recycled paper

Library of Congress Catalog Card Number 95-78195

ISBN 0-9620812-9-9

Dedicated to
MRS. SOHAKU OGATA (Ogata Fujin),
wife of the late priest and head of Chotoku-in at Shokoku-ji
in Kyoto. She is one of the great Zen people I have met,
and I am indeed grateful to her.

Contents

Foreword to New Edition

Twenty years after first writing this book, I find I am still in agreement with what it says. After one trip to Japan I reported to Roshi Joshu Sasaki what I had found. He remarked that "in fifty years there won't be any *real* Zen in Japan." I answered that it would not take that long. Why? Because it seemed to him (and to me) that the emphasis was being placed on the finger pointing at the moon and the moon was being ignored. Continuous emphasis on routine, gongs, bells, and everything else sometimes seems more like "churchianity" than the discipline that Hui-neng polished for the world. When visiting Dogen's Eiheiji temple in the cold mountains, I felt that the monks had little time for concentration, being too busy sweeping out rooms and taking cash from the visitors (who watched Zen movies in midday, while this poor fool sat Zazen with the monks at 3:30 a.m.). Since I have great reverence for Dogen Zenji, the founder of Soto Zen in Japan, I can picture him turning over in his resting place. His act of returning half a dipperful of water to the river before he drank would not be understood, or even noticed (what is wrong with returning to you that which is originally yours?).

It has been said that Zen is without objective. One monk, when I asked why he sat Zazen and studied Buddhism, answered, "I don't know." I greatly respected his answer. Another, when I noted that he was putting on weight (hard to do on monastery food!), said drily, "I was too light; I used to blow around." So seeking nothing, he was able to anchor himself. Dogen said, "I found I had a nose in the center of my face."

In truth, Zen adherents want to experience "Kensho," seeing into one's own nature. When it happens, there is no doubt about it. Writers speak of "instant enlightenment," sudden and incomprehensible "Satori" (enlightenment), but the monk or lay person may have practiced for twenty years leading up to this sudden realization. Zen, however, is not a practice of stages, no matter how many times I have heard these stages defined by Zen "officials" who have not themselves experienced realization. They are speaking from what they have read and what they have heard. "Do not be misled by others," one adept admonished himself each day, and he then answered, "Yes sir, yes sir, I won't."

Zen greatly admires "attaining nothing," which means progressing without aiming at a destination. This nothing grows into what I have called "the growth of certainty" in another book.* Since it is nothing, it cannot be lost.

When Chao Chou (Joshu) was asked, "If a man comes here carrying nothing, what should I tell him?" Chao Chou answered, "Tell him to throw it out!" There is more to the exchange, but it is enough that Chao Chou warns that one should not cling even to enlightenment (emptiness), but forget it and go on to work for others — this is proceeding on from the top of a hundred-foot pole. How can a master find "him or herself" (in the smaller sense), when he or she no longer has a self? "Carrying nothing" means taking the bucket to the well and bringing back water for the others.

The words "emptiness" and "void" occur so often in Zen that it is necessary to remember that they do not mean a lack of anything; the sky, mountains, trees, and dust of the city are still

---

Abandon Hope/The Way to Fulfillment

there. But all things are empty of self-nature, void of a permanent identity. Each is dependent on the other. When we think of the three principles of Buddhism — Annica (impermanence), Dukkha (suffering), and Anatta (no lasting self, no permanent identity) — we must remember that even they are empty of self-nature.

"Prajna" is a term denoting "inherent wisdom," and it often sounds like a euphemism for some people's concept of God or the Chinese idea of Tao. It is to be experienced, not defined. When one lives from Prajna, he or she will find inspiration and guidance. Don't believe it, just experience it.

Hopefully, the above ramblings make some sense to the inexperienced, who may find great "Nothing" in Zen practice.

Introduction

When my publisher asked me to write a book on "Zen Meditation," I was somewhat dubious about doing so. There had been many books written on this subject, usually limited to the sitting practice known as "Zazen," and I did not see why I should add to the deluge. After considering the matter for awhile, however, I realized that "Zen Meditation" meant something more to me than just cross-legged sitting. With a previous book of mine, *The Joys of Meditation*, we had noticed how eager readers were for actual instruction in how to practice rather than for abstruse musings about meditation, no matter how profound. Most people want to practice, and most books want to expound philosophy or some special point of view, so the two do not always come together. Accordingly, I agreed to attempt the book on "Zen Meditation," adding the phrase "A Broad View" to explain what the real purposes of the book are.

Most people who study or practice Zen in the West know only the terminology and teachings of Japanese Zen. Some go to the Orient, and, naturally, visit Japanese Zen temples. For political reasons, we do not associate China with Zen practice today and look to Japanese teachers and writers for our information. However, Zen was a Chinese development, and "The Golden Age of Zen" took place in China, beginning over a thousand years ago. Many of the advanced practices of the Ts'ao

Tung (Japanese: Soto) and Lin-Chi (Japanese: Rinzai) sects are
not taught in Japan today. When the great schools of Chinese
Ch'an (Zen) came across the water to Nippon, inexplicably some
of the great teachings were left behind. The four-fold meditation
of Lin-Chi (Rinzai), having to do with subject and object, is not
generally taught in present-day Japan. Dogen Zenji, founder of
the Japanese Soto sect, was undoubtedly aware of both the Koan
practice (which he had participated in before going to China) and
the "Five Ranks" of his own school on the Mainland, but he did
not use either in is teaching at Eihei-ji, the central temple of Soto
Zen where Dogen taught for so many years. It is said that he
thought Koan practice led to mere "dialectics," and the teachings
of the "Five Ranks" was too esoteric for his taste. In his
writings, Dogen continually stressed Zazen, cross-legged
meditation, in preference to other methods available in this book.

   To a practitioner and a meditator, it must always be
stressed that Zen is Zen Buddhism. A monk without inherent
faith in his Buddha Nature will find it hard to make progress.
Just sitting, without sitting in the Buddhist sense, may offer
certain powers (there are those who "just sit" in Japan, very often
artisans who receive inspiration from sitting), but it is not the
practice of Zen Buddhism. We will start by assuming that the
reader has a little deeper view of life than the average person,
who may just be interested in eating, sleeping, making a living,
and finding some pleasure while he or she lives. Too soon, the
person's life passes by without being in the least meaningful, and
if the circumstances of that life change drastically from pleasant
to unpleasant, that one is apt to be bewildered and blame some
whimsical God who has made this happen to him or her. Most
are at the mercy of circumstances without realizing that they,
themselves, have caused those circumstances. It is amazing how
few grasp the meaning of cause and effect. It is common to
believe that fortune and also misfortune drop like manna from the
sky, without any reason. When we are prosperous, it is because

we are clever. When misfortune overtakes us, however, we are "unlucky." Seldom does it occur to us to take responsibility for what happens to us. Many have heard the word "Karma," but few want to accept the fruits of Karma. When we do accept responsibility for what happens to us, both pleasant and unpleasant, a great patience develops and we are careful of what we do and say in the present as we realize we are now forming the future.

So we may assume that the reader is one who is interested in something besides the animal appetites. If he or she is not vitally concerned with life and death, yet there is something of an "ultimate concern" at the back of his or her consciousness. He or she wants some answers, dimly knowing that those answers may not come in words. We are all seekers of "Truth," whether we look for it in drink, in crime, or in perverse sex. The one who is beginning to shop around for a meditation, for a movement, or for a teaching may be still a dilettante but is headed in a positive direction. Once that person begins to practice, in however desultory a manner, he or she has "entered the stream" in Buddhist terminology — he or she has made a beginning. Though it may take many, many lives, he or she will eventually reach the shore of Enlightenment and come into his or her heritage of undifferentiated Joy.

The doctrine of "many lives" is, of course, vital to Buddhism, as it is to all Indian thought. If Time is considered as a circle, rather than a linear measurement from beginning to end, one will be able to grasp the significance of endless aeons of Time, constantly moving in a cyclical manner. The Japanese Master Dogen is quoted as saying: "Time does not have a separate existence; it is established by existence." This might be from the mouth of the Buddha himself. However, this relativity of Time is not apparent to most of us. We believe time is something absolute, and this makes it difficult for us to grasp the transitory nature of life.

"Spring draws in the flowers, and the flowers draw in Spring," said Dogen, thus admirably illustrating the interdependence of all modes of existence. This arises because that has arisen; and that exists because of this. This mutual dependence and mutual origination is at the very heart of the Buddhist enlightenment, in which it is finally realized that things do not have their own immutable self-nature but depend on everything else. This will bring a great understanding of the Buddhist doctrine of "Sunyata" or Void. This "Void" is not emptiness in the ordinary sense, a vacuity with a lack of anything. In one religion it may be thought of as "the Great Emptiness" and in another, "the Great Fullness." In either case, it is without aspects, containing all without any discernable characteristics of its own. If we wish, we can call it God. "God" or "Sunyata," these are just words. When we have the experience, we will not wish to label it.

It is not necessary for the beginning meditator, or even the experienced one, to understand the difficult points mentioned above. In this book all will receive instruction in how to pursue Zen Meditation in the broader sense. It is desirable that one sit Zazen in the prescribed manner, but cross-legged sitting is not all there is to Zen Meditation. What is important is that the meditator develop his or her own insights, that one does not believe something because somebody else tells one to. Your Zen must be "Your Zen," not just an echo.

It is really amazing how many Zen people have been creative. Though there were relatively few Zen adherents in Japan, all Japanese art and aesthetic practices seem to have proceeded from the Zen awakening. In China we find the great landscapes of Zen and Taoist artists and the cogent insights of the beautiful poetry written by Ch'an monks and adepts. We cannot even call these expressions "religious" in the ordinary sense; they are too full of life to be limited by a category. A

Zen poet (in Dr. Chang Chung Yuan's excellent translation of a monk's poem) says:

> I gather chrysanthemums at the eastern hedgerow,
> And silently gaze at the southern mountains.
> The mountain air is beautiful in the sunset,
> And the birds, flocking together, return home.
> Among all these things is a real meaning,
> Yet, when I try to express it, I become lost in "no-words."

Here is the description of "Suchness," that-which-is. It cannot be subsumed under any category; it is the Life Force itself. But how apparent that the poet has arrived at some insight! We would surmise that he has spent long hours in meditation, realizing the self by forgetting the self. When, as Hakuin stated, "From that time on, things of the world were viewed like the back of my own hand," the meditator has realized his identity as the self of all things. This is the great emptiness, or the great fullness, with no room for the little, limited, conditioned ego-sense that plagues us all.

So begin your Zen Meditation. According to what you give to it, there will be rewards, perhaps far beyond what is expected. But it must be done regularly and assiduously. When teaching "Comparative Meditation" or "T'ai Chi Ch'uan" at universities, I have, as teacher, often been overwhelmed by the initial enthusiasm of the students. Those who are wildly enthusiastic on the third day may have dropped out by the tenth day. I tell my students I am not impressed by enthusiasm. When they ask what will impress me, I answer: "Steadfastness." That means practicing on the days one feels like it and also practicing when one doesn't feel like it. It means eliminating activities and diversions which interfere with regular practice. If the reader sincerely wants to meditate and attain something, even though that something may be the "great nothing of Zen," he must be willing to pay the price. Zen practice is not for infants or panty-waists. Once having recognized that, it only remains to "do it."

If the reader is able to practice under a Zen Master, he or she is fortunate and should pursue such good fortune assiduously. There are apt to be fewer false prophets and poseurs in Zen than in the fields of Yoga; or at least that is my conclusion. Zen practice is not as glamorous, and Zen sitting is difficult and sometimes painful. Those who are not really serious tend to drop by the wayside. If it is possible to study under a master, by all means do so. If not, one can use the limited instruction of this not very worthy book to go one's own way. The rewards will be there, and meditation itself is a great reward, if only we realize it.

The Lotus Sutra says: "In the State of Emptiness, each man's body is a body filling the Universe, his voice is a voice overflowing the Cosmos, and his life is a life which is without limit."

This is a glorious message and a true one. Through Zen meditation, its truth can be experienced. As a taster knows whether the water is hot or cold, so does the experiencer, without doubt, come to realize the True Meaning. Turning back one's though on itself, carrying on one's thinking without thinking, one arrives at a point where no more can be jettisoned, and then one has arrived at the Source.

What is Zen Meditation?
Zen Meditation is NOW-NESS.
How does one realize this NOW?
By harmonizing mind and body.
How does one harmonize mind and body?
By forgetting mind and body.
In what way is the self realized?
By forgetting the self, the self is realized.

Chapter 1
ALL BEINGS ARE PRIMARILY BUDDHAS
(it is like water and ice)

The term "Zen Meditation" does not only refer to cross-legged sitting known as "Zazen." In truth, the word "Zen" itself means Meditation. It is generally agreed that "Zen" is the Japanese reading for the Chinese characters pronounced "Ch'anna" (or "Ch'an"), and Ch'anna is the closest the Chinese can come to pronouncing the Sanskrit "Dhyana" or Pali "Jhana," both of which mean Indian-style meditation. So "Zen" is the meditation sect of Buddhism, as opposed to other sects which depend upon philosophy, repetition of the Buddha's name, abstruse negation, and dialectics. Zen Meditation, far from being just a period of cross-legged sitting, refers to the "twenty-four-hour awareness" that is the goal of the adept. Brushing the teeth is Zazen, losing the temper is Zazen, and human communication is Zazen. When the daily activities of life, such as drinking tea and taking a bath, are performed with an empty heart, they are perfect examples of Zen Meditation in the broader sense. And sitting cross-legged for long periods of time after eating only one meal a day and observing the precepts is not true meditation if it is done with a seething inside and a grasping heart.

Zen supposedly came to China in the sixth century, brought there by the great Indian, Bodhidharma. Truthfully, there had been no "Zen" as such in India, and later records of

Zen patriarchs reaching all the way back to Mahakasyapa and the Buddha himself are probably apocryphal. Zen is primarily a Chinese development, and the teaching Bodhidharma brought from India was cross-fertilized by the indigenous Taoism of China. So Zen is the child of the wedding between Indian Buddhism and Chinese Taoism. The "Wu Wei" of the latter helped form the distinctly Chinese character of the former, just as Zen later was responsible for preserving Taoism in China at a time when it appeared to be dying out.

We do not know whether Bodhidharma, in the years he sat facing a wall at Shaolin Temple, closed his eyes and practiced trance in the Indian fashion. This was the "Dhyana" of India, to focus the mind on one point, whether a mantra or a visualization, until the mind became one-pointed and then no-pointed, entering a trance-like state in which there was no sound, no sight, and no sensual consciousness at all. This was the preliminary to the Indian state of Samadhi, the "super-conscious" condition that was so much different from the Zen Samadhi we later heard about.

We do know that a great many years later, the Sixth Patriarch's contemporary, Shen-hsiu, was still teaching the type of Dhyana in the "Northern School" of Zen. He thought of it as a contemplation of Purity, which certainly corresponded to the traditional Indian view of meditation, and in his famous gatha presented to the Fifth Patriarch, spoke of "wiping the mirror clean" so that no dust could accumulate. This is far from the view of Ultimate Emptiness later expressed by Hui-neng, the Sixth Patriarch, and seems to present good reason to believe that, in the seventh century, traditional Indian meditation was still being taught as "Zen" in China. It was during the time of the Sixth Patriarch that radical changes came over Zen practice, that the Indian influences were wiped out, and Zen developed into a true Chinese way.

Buddhism, of course, had reached China long before Bodhidharma, and many Sutras (scriptures, spoken by the

Buddha) had already been translated into the Chinese language. When Bodhidharma faced the Chinese emperor (what language did they speak?) he was facing a man who had some knowledge of scriptural Buddhism and who attempted to put into practice the principles derived therefrom. He was well-versed in traditional Buddhism, but judging by the dialogue with the great Master Bodhidharma, not at all ready for the deeper Zen meanings.

Actually, Zen, as we know it today, really started with Hui-neng, the Sixth Patriarch. Many feel it died at the end of the T'ang Dynasty in China, often called the Golden Age of Zen. Certainly much of what was practiced in this Golden Age never reached Japan, and the Zen practiced in Japanese temples today leans heavily on the motionless sitting known as Zazen, sometimes, as in much of Soto Zen, to the exclusion of everything else. But this was not the Chinese teaching of meditation as conveyed by the earlier Chinese Zen Masters. Hui-neng, in his "Altar Sutra" (also known as "The Scripture of the Sixth Patriarch") said that such continued "quiet-sitting" was not Zen but a disease. He had no sympathy for "quiescence" and wanted the Prajna Wisdom to shine forth spontaneously from the mind, which was empty while in the midst of activity. His "meditation" was not a way of being without thought but of not being attached to the thoughts as they arose. Such spontaneity seems to have been largely lost in the Zen temples of today in Japan.

A subtler criticism of the quietistic approach to Zen Enlightenment occurs when the great Master Huai-jang, coming upon Ma-tsu in seclusion high in the mountains, asked: "What does your Reverence hope to gain from such sitting?"

"I hope to become a Buddha," was the answer.

Then the Master picked up a flat-surfaced stone and began rubbing it. Curious as to the reason why the Master was performing this strange act, the other asked for an explanation.

"To make it into a mirror by polishing it," was the instant answer.

Amused, the hermit-monk asked: "How can you make a stone into a mirror by polishing it?"

"And how can you become a Buddha by sitting?" was the sharp rejoinder.

There are, of course, many levels to this profound dialogue. The Master was not decrying sitting meditation as such, as some non-practicing writers have claimed. He was simply pointing out that, if the stone was not a mirror to begin with, it could not become one and that the sitting mountain monk could only "become" a Buddha if he *already* was one. He was pointing directly at the Buddha Nature, not to be won by endless quiet sitting when, in truth, it was already possessed and manifested!

Still, this dialogue points the difference between the true practice of Zen Meditation and the mistaken piling-up-of-hours sitting cross-legged, much like a student accumulating flight time on his or her way to a commercial pilot's license. If the sitter does not realize his or her Essential Nature, long hours of quiet sitting are not apt to do the trick. As Hui-neng pointed out, the Prajna Wisdom must flash out in the mind, like lightning revealing the hitherto-darkened landscape. Certainly Zazen, in the periods of cross-legged sitting, can help in the overall practice, but it is not, in itself, true Zen Meditation. It is doubtful if the illiterate Hui-neng, who had never been a monk at the time he was made Sixth Patriarch, ever sat cross-legged Zazen in his life. His first experience of illumination came when he heard someone reading a passage from the "Diamond Sutra" about the "mind that abides nowhere." Such a statement wipes out the general concept of an eternal Absolute. It sweeps away God in an absolute sense, leaving the listener with nothing to lean on and not a thing on which to depend, precisely the condition for which Zen Meditation aims.

If sitting cross-legged would, in itself, lead to enlighten-ment, most of the people of India would be enlightened, as they customarily sit this way. There is no doubt, however, that formal Zazen — that is, long periods of cross-legged sitting interspersed with walking and chanting — is an important part of Zen practice in all temples, and many practice it alone. Whether working on the Koan problem (as in Rinzai Zen), watching the mind itself (observing the thinking process), or "just sitting," as in Shikan-Taza, definite physiological changes take place in the experienced sitter and one can reach a condition of great Joy, of utter Emptiness, or great Equanimity by practicing this kind of Zazen. And it is sitting in the NOW! Day-dreaming, memory or wishful thinking, as well as prayer and pietistic musing, have no part in sitting practice. We are here NOW, in the world as it is NOW. There is no Buddha apart from Beings, and no Beings apart from Buddha, we do not have to concern ourselves with some transcendental state that dualistically places us apart from this life. It is all here, now, in Zen, and we must grasp this obvious fact in order to practice Zen Meditation and let our Essential Nature shine through.

Hakuin's "Dhyana Wasson" (Song of Meditation) clearly illustrates the broader meaning of Zen Meditation, and it is a thrilling work. In the eighteenth century in Japan, Hakuin Zenji began to revive the dying Zen, and all lines of descent in Rinzai Zen come through this mystic Master, who was certainly one of the two great Zen influences in Japan. In Professor Ogata's fine translation, Hakuin says:

ALL BEINGS ARE PRIMARILY BUDDHAS:
IT IS LIKE WATER AND ICE.
THERE IS NO ICE APART FROM WATER:
THERE ARE NO BUDDHAS APART FROM BEINGS.
NOT KNOWING HOW CLOSE THE TRUTH IS TO
        THEM,
BEINGS SEEK FOR IT AFAR — WHAT A PITY!

THEY ARE LIKE THOSE WHO, BEING IN THE
      MIDST OF WATER,
CRY OUT FOR WATER, FEELING THIRST.

THOSE WHO, FOR ONCE,
LISTENING TO THE DHARMA,
IN ALL HUMILITY PRAISE IT AND FAITHFULLY
      FOLLOW IT,
WILL BE ENDOWED WITH INNUMERABLE
      MERITS.
BUT HOW MUCH MORE SO
WHEN YOU TURN YOUR EYES WITHIN YOUR
      SELVES,
AND HAVE A GLIMPSE INTO YOUR OWN SELF-
      NATURE!
YOU FIND THAT THE SELF-NATURE IS NO
      NATURE —
THE TRUTH PERMITTING NO IDLE SOPHISTRY.
FOR YOU THEN OPENS THE GATE LEADING TO
THE ONENESS OF CAUSE AND EFFECT:
BEFORE YOU THEN LIES
A STRAIGHT ROAD OF NON-DUALITY AND NON-
      TRINITY.

WHEN YOU COME TO UNDERSTAND
THAT FORM IS THE FORM OF THE FORMLESS,
YOUR COMING AND GOING
TAKE PLACE NOWHERE ELSE BUT WHERE YOU
      ARE.
WHEN YOU UNDERSTAND THAT
THOUGHT IS THE THOUGHT OF THE THOUGHT
      LESS,
YOUR SINGING AND DANCING IS
NO OTHER THAN THE VOICE OF THE DHARMA.

HOW BOUNDLESS IS THE SKY OF SAMADHI!
HOW REFRESHINGLY BRIGHT
IS THE MOON OF THE FOURFOLD WISDOM!
BEING SO, IS THERE ANYTHING YOU LACK?
AS THE ABSOLUTE PRESENTS ITSELF BEFORE
        YOU,
THE PLACE WHERE YOU STAND
IS THE LAND OF THE LOTUS,
AND YOUR PERSON,
THE BODY OF THE BUDDHA.

Chapter 2
STILL-SITTING
(the purpose of Zazen is not to be quiet,
but to let your True Nature manifest)

In India, most so-called holy men sit in the Full Lotus Posture, with each leg up on the opposite thigh. This pose seems easy for the Indian people, and I have never seen a meditator using a pillow, as in Japan and America. Practically all pictures and statues of the Buddha show him sitting easily in this pose, his hands forming different significant Mudras (positions) which speak clearly to scholars and teachers. In such a pose it is stressed that the backbone be held straight. In India, of course, it was the custom for the meditator to close his or her eyes, in contrast to the slightly-opened eyes of the Zazen sitter in Japan and America today. This Full Lotus position securely anchors the meditator against falling. He or she does not have to worry that, if going into a deep state or even falling asleep, he or she will topple over and get hurt. So the Full Lotus Pose is the best, if one is able to attain and hold it.

However, even in Japan and China, such a posture is very difficult for the lay person and also for many monks. For this reason, in temples, permission is usually granted for the sitter to take the Half Lotus position, in which only one leg is placed upon the opposite thigh. If this position is taken, the Soto Zen temples of Japan demand that the sitter place the left foot on top, with the right foot being underneath. Such customs may vary from temple to temple, but generally, Soto Zen wants the left foot on top, for reasons which sound vague and not at all convincing. Probably the original reason has been lost, just as the rationale has been lost behind the great Dogen Zenji's returning half a dipper of water to the river every time he scooped it up. No matter. If one is sitting in the Rinzai school, no great fuss is made as to which leg is on top (providing the meditator is sitting properly), while Soto does want the left leg to predominate. Similarly, in Kinhin, the walking period between spells of cross-legged sitting, Soto puts the right hand on top of the left, at the chest, and Rinzai reverses this by placing the left hand on top. The main points in sitting are to keep the back straight, the sternum up, and the knees on the ground so that one is making a three-pointed stance with the knees at two ends of the triangle, balancing the Tanden (T'an T'ien in Chinese), the important spot two inches below the navel. Rinzai Zen makes much of the breathing, with this Tanden as the focus, but Soto does not pay much attention to it.

Zen Masters placed great value on the Full Lotus position for themselves, as will be noted in the following story:

Most Zen Masters easily predicted the time of their own death; they bathed, had their heads shaven, and sat in Full Lotus position as they were about to pass away — often writing the traditional four-line gatha (a poem expressing their insight) before they left this world. There was one Zen Master, however, who had been disabled most of his life, and he was unable to sit in this Full Lotus pose all the years he taught his disciples.

When the time for death approached, this courageous man, with his own hands, broke his own leg and pulled it up on his thigh so he was sitting in the desired position. One can imagine the agony he underwent! It is not difficult to envision the bone of the leg breaking through the skin and spilling blood all over the matting. The awed monks, after watching this titanic

Figure 1

exhibition, never washed away the bloodstains, leaving them there for future generations to see and ponder on. Such is the stuff of which a true Zen person is made!

Because it is difficult for modern meditators, even in the Eastern part of the Orient, to sit in the Full Lotus position, or even the Half Lotus, it has become acceptable for most to sit in a way that is uniquely Zen's (see Figure 1). Here one leg is flat on the floor, extended to one side, and the other leg is placed flat upon the first, with the foot turned up and nestling in the corner of the thigh. This almost gives the appearance of the Half Lotus posture. There is a problem, as one leg is higher than the other, in having both knees touch the ground at the same time, and the beginning sitter will have to adjust for this when starting to sit.

Monks in both Soto and Rinzai Zen usually sit on a raised platform. There is a round pillow called a "Zafu" on which they sit, though in some zendos and temples in America ordinary pillows are used. Naturally, the higher the sitter is placed, the easier and more comfortable will be the position, but if the seat is too high, there is the danger of toppling forward.

Rinzai Zen sitters take their place facing the center of the room. That is, they are actually facing each other. (In Japan we do not see monks and nuns sitting in the same place, absolute segregation of the sexes being practiced. However, in this country, and with lay people in Japan, men and women are frequently mixed together.)

Soto Zen feels that sitting facing other sitters can be distracting, though the eyes are fastened rigidly on the ground a few feet ahead and one should not be aware of the others. Therefore, Soto has the sitters turned to the opposite direction, facing the wall. This does have a more private and intimate feeling and is said to duplicate the position of the First Zen Patriarch, Bodhidharma, who was called the "Wall-Gazing Brahmin" because he sat facing the wall for nine years at Shaolin Temple. This wall, of course, has great symbolic meaning, and

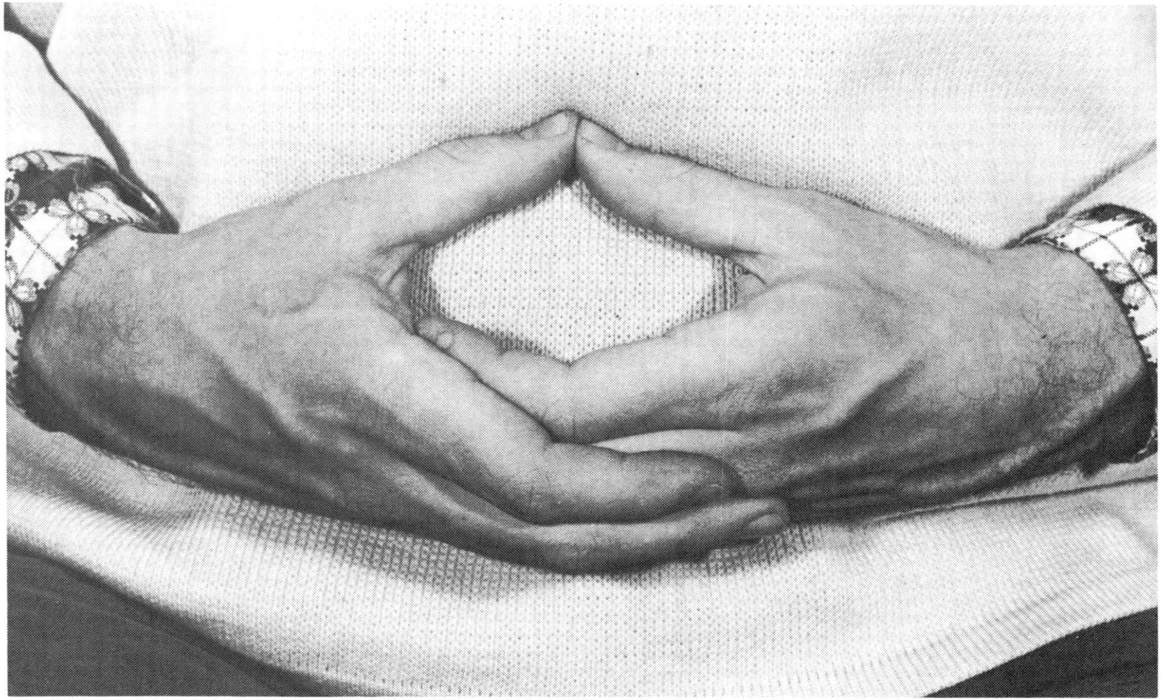

Figure 2

I am sure the real point of the Bodhidharma story is somewhat esoteric. One must break through this wall, which is the self-enclosed ego center that limits and conditions our lives.

Thus, Soto sitters face the wall and Rinzai sitters face each other. There is a slightly different emphasis on which leg must be on top and on the hand positions taken during the walking Kinhin. As we shall see, there is a great deal of difference as to what the Soto monk is doing, mentally, from what the Rinzai monk, or student, is supposed to be doing.

When one has seated oneself on the pillow or pillows, he or she makes the correct hand position. Some Chinese monks sat in the Taoist manner, with the two thumbs crossed, one digging into the palm of the other hand to form a connection for the meridian channels (as in acupuncture) so that the Chi (Prana) could flow uninterruptedly during the sitting. I have seen pictures of monks in Japanese temples holding their hands this way. However, wherever I have sat in Japan, I have noticed lay people, beginners, and monks all making the preferred mudra that brings the tips of the two thumbs together.

In this hand position, we place the left hand, fingers together, on top of the right hand slightly below the belt level. Turning the two hands palms up, we dig the edge of the hands into the belly. Then, raising the two thumbs (held apart from the other fingers), we press the tips of the thumbs against each other. This position can be observed in Figure 2 and is known as "Inzo" in Japanese.

This places the focus of concentration on the spot below the navel known as "Tanden," mentioned earlier in this chapter. One great Zen Master said that it is there, down at the Tanden, that the monks will "find the secret of the Universe." Another pointed out that this mudra will expand until it encompasses the universe. When Zen Master Dogen, in the thirteenth century, went to China to study and practice, he entered the room of his Master, Ju-ching, for instruction. The latter simply said, "Dogen, when sitting in meditation, place your consciousness on your left hand." This, in effect, was placing his concentration on the Tanden (T'an T'ien) below the navel, the spot that is so important in all Chinese and Japanese disciplines. From this instruction came the Soto Shikan-Taza ("Nothing but Sitting"), where there is no Koan and no other focus of thought, the concentration on the Tanden being itself the thought. This is the preferred way of sitting for Soto lay persons and monks today.

In the Soto tradition, sitters sway back and forth after they are on the pillows. This has the same effect as stretching. Rinzai sitters are free to make such easing motions if they want, but it is not prescribed for them.

Once one has taken a firm seat and made the proper hand mudra, he or she should place the tongue against the palate (roof) of the mouth and open the nostrils wide. This last is important, and it is the reason many Zen sitters give a fierce appearance. The widening of the nostrils gives the face an awesome expression, certainly not incompatible with Zen practice. One does not sit Zazen in steam-heated comfort. Often have I, at Shokoku-ji in Kyoto, heard the monks begin their sitting in the meditation hall at midnight on a cold winter evening. The doors at the end of the meditation hall are usually left open, and a breeze sweeps through the room. This is comfortable in summer and freezing in winter. The monks do not wear socks or shoes (though white tabi, the traditional Japanese foot covering, are acceptable). With the nostrils wide open, the good air is breathed in. Certainly the pranic content is all-important (Prana being the Chinese "Chi," "Ki" in Japanese). Those who sit Zazen in warm, steam-heated places can hurt themselves.

It is interesting, too, that if one sits correctly, breathes in the air, and keeps the focus on the Tanden two inches below the navel, he or she will not be cold during the sitting. It is my feeling that T'ai Chi Ch'uan and T'ai Chi Chih could be utilized for the purpose of getting the Prana to flow before the sitting, but this is not done in Japan. Hakuin Zenji, in his famous "Yasen-kanna," does point out a way to circulate the Ki energy, making the sitter oblivious to cold (as with the naked Yogis in northern India and Tibet), but it seems to have disappeared in present-day Japan, more's the pity. This Nai Kan* (Nei Kung in Chinese) is very valuable and, according to Hakuin's own account, helped him in his breakthrough to Zen enlightenment.

Living in a freezing Zen sub-temple in Kyoto during the cold winter months (there is no heat, the sun does not reach the temple rooms, and there is an interior garden, which is aesthetically very pleasing but brings ice and snow right into the inside), I found it favorable to do certain breathings and mental circulation of the Chi (Ki, Prana) before beginning to sit. While the breath is held at the top of the circle (or at the bottom*), there is no feeling of cold whatsoever. Thoughts tend to stop when the breath is held, and I was able to create a body warmth before beginning meditation (Zazen) in my small room. When there is no thought, of course, there is no apperception. I do believe circulation of the Vital Force, before sitting, can be a very helpful tool for Zazen.

With the tongue pressed against the roof of the mouth and the nostrils held open (so that the ends of the mouth tend to drop slightly), the sitter focuses his or her gaze along the nose and lets it come to rest a few feet in front of him or herself, on the floor mat. If facing a wall, undoubtedly one will be gazing intently at some spot on the wall. The eyes are to be kept half-

---

*See the author's *Meditation for Healing/Particular Meditations for Particular Results* for description and instruction in the "Nei Kung" and *T'ai Chi Chih/Joy thru Movement* for description and instruction in "Great Circle Meditation."

open in Zen Meditation. Moreover, while the eyes are gazing intently at a spot, the concentration is not on that object. Zazen is an ingoing practice. Gazing at a place on the floor or a spot on the wall, one is oblivious of that point of focus. We are looking within in Zazen. One American who has spent more than twelve years in Kyoto studying Rinzai Zen swears that all the Masters meditate with their eyes closed. Be that as it may, the student and disciple are instructed to gaze down along the nose, keeping the eyes slightly open at all times (so that one will not go off into "unrecordable" states).

In a Zen temple, one monk will usually circle the Zendo slowly, with a stick known as "kyosaku" on his shoulder, during meditation periods. He is usually authorized to use the stick whenever necessary to snap the sitter out of any undesirable condition. He also corrects the posture of anyone sitting poorly. This use of the stick — hitting twice on one side of the neck and twice on the other — is not punishment. Usually the striker will make enough noise in hitting to startle those sitting nearby, which is not considered a bad thing. A sharp, quick pain, such as an experienced striker gives, can revitalize a sluggish or tired system, and some sitters actually ask for the striking by placing their two hands together as the monk with the stick walks by. For a newcomer, of course, the appearance of the walking monk on the periphery of vision can be a frightening experience. The experienced sitter ignores him.

The length of one sitting is usually determined by the burning of a piece of incense. At home, a lay person might want to make each period thirty or forty minutes, which might correspond to the average time that it takes the incense to burn down.

In a temple, between spells of sitting, the monks form a line and walk, usually outside the meditation hall. Sometimes they chant while walking, but this is relatively rare and demands that each know the chanted Sutra perfectly, as it is difficult to repeat the sounds as slowly as one walks. I have noticed that Soto Zen tends to walk in a very leisurely fashion, each foot being drawn up to the other in a seeming-hesitation step, while Rinzai Zen sitters may walk more rapidly, depending on the mood of the one leading Kinhin. This book is obviously not being written for monks, and it is suggested that beginners set their own period of Kinhin after sitting motionless for too long a time. It is important for the intrinsic energy (Chi, Ki) to flow again, and circulation of the blood that will follow such flow will help to alleviate the pain of cramped legs. It is not at all unusual for the sitter's legs to go to sleep during a period of Zazen, and the walking helps restore a healthier condition. When there is chanting (such as the Heart Sutra) during Kinhin, I have found it very powerful. Often, for this one chanter, it has felt as though the right side of the head, down through the ear, was about to split open. This feeling always stopped immediately after the Sutra was completed.

During the walking period, the walker stays in step and keeps the eyes focused on the feet of the one walking in front of him or her. The object of concentration is maintained; it is now simply a walking meditation. If one is walking alone, he or she should fold the hands at the chest (right hand on top for Soto, left hand for Rinzai) and keep the concentration while walking at an even pace. Three to five minutes of Kinhin (walking) might be sufficient to offset thirty minutes of sitting.

Experienced sitters will often feel an unexplained vibration in the ankles or below the belt. Sometimes it reaches up to the nape of the neck and the hairs seem to stand on end. These are good signs, showing the Vital Force is circulating and, in other forms of Chinese meditation, such manifestations are looked on as being healing in nature.

So much for the sitting posture. Japanese Zen Masters today make much of the correct way to sit. Westerners usually spend one year in Japan learning to sit correctly, instructed by a monk, before they meet a Rinzai Zen Roshi (Master) who will give them a Koan problem to work on. Even then, there is a difficulty as very few Zen Masters speak foreign languages, and Sanzen (the "Kill-or-be-Killed" personal confrontation with the Master when one is working on a Koan) demands communication. An interpreter is absolutely "non grata" as he or she would tend to deaden the spontaneity necessary in Zen practice. It would be best for future Zen students to study the Japanese (or Chinese) language before going to the Orient, continuing to try to master the language while perfecting the sitting. I often wonder how Dogen and other Japanese monks who went to China, in ancient days, managed to communicate with their masters at the outset.

To reiterate: all Zazen instructors insist that the back be held straight, that the sternum be thrust out, that the shoulders be relaxed, and that both knees touch the ground. The open eyes are lowered slightly and focused on a spot a few feet ahead. The hand mudra is held firmly, and the head is slightly inclined to the front, while being held back on the neck in a firm posture that looks somewhat like a cadet "bracing." One does not droop during Zazen; care should be taken that the posture is firm, no matter how painful the legs may temporarily become.

It must be stressed that one should not do Zazen or any form of meditation immediately after meals. The breathing slows down in Zazen and there will not be proper oxidation in the system to help with digestion. Almost all monks I have met in Japan have suffered from stomach trouble, probably because of the soft diet, the relatively poor quality of the food (Zen temples are not rich, and Zen teaching makes much of "poverty"), and the habit of sitting long meditations too soon after meals.

Chapter 3
WATCHING THE MIND
(when thought disappears, where is this mind?)

The attitude with which Rinzai Zen students approach Zen Meditation is quite different from that of Soto Zen students. The former usually work with a Koan, the problem given them by the Zen Master, and their training requires occasional contact with that Master in Sanzen, the face-to-face confrontation in which the student states (or manifests) his or her understanding of the Koan. It is true that there have been examples of solitary meditators who have, themselves, worked with a well-known Koan, such as, "If all things are reducible to the One, to what is the One reducible?" However, this is relatively rare, and Koan practice in Rinzai Zen usually necessitates contact with the Master.

Koan practice can be the most frustrating thing in the world. It is a great ego-crusher. Traditionally, continued Koan practice tends to raise a great doubt in the meditator's mind, this doubt being called I Chin(g) in Chinese. Actually, it is a mass that grows up in the subconscious and stays with the meditator during all his or her activities. The greater the doubt, the greater the enlightenment experience (Satori in Japanese, Wu in Chinese), it is said. When the doubt finally bursts, all questions are resolved in the moment of the Great Joy (usually accompanied by tears and perspiration). So the purpose of Rinzai Zen training is to arouse this doubt and to bring about one-pointedness of mind, thus hastening the enlightenment experience. It is said that a Zen student without Satori is just one who consumes food and wastes the Master's time. The only way he or she can pay back the Master's kindness is to have the Great Experience, and then go on to surpass the Master and carry on the teacher's Zen.

Whereas Rinzai Zen students are frankly pursuing Satori, Soto Zen meditators have a different attitude. It is felt that sitting (Zazen) is simply the expression of their Buddha Nature, without any striving whatsoever. The true Soto person is just grateful to be allowed to practice. In what is sometimes referred to as "The Genjo Koan," Soto Zen followers believe that this world, just as it is, is their ideal world. As one Soto teacher said to me, "Life itself is enough of a Koan." Therefore, the Soto Zen meditator sits to express his or her Original Nature, seeking nothing. Dogen Zenji, founder of Soto Zen in Japan, stated, "Do not feel that you will necessarily be aware of your own enlightenment." Sitting is just sitting, not a means to any end.

In truth, however, Soto Zen students often have had some experience in Rinzai Zen training, and vice-versa. There is no doubt that, whatever he or she may say, the Soto Zen student is pursuing Enlightenment. Therefore, the practice is a means to an end, though the student is often cautioned against pursuing goals. The aim of a Zen follower is to be free of all conditioning, and any ambition is, itself, a conditioning agent.

The continued reference to "Soto Zen" and "Rinzai Zen" may be confusing to the reader. Originally, there were five great schools of Zen (Ch'an) training in China. Some of these, such as the profound Hogen school, came to Japan but did not prosper on the native soil and died out. So today, we have two great schools left in Japan, as repositories of Zen Buddhist training. They are "Soto," derived from the "Ts'ao-Tung" school in China, with about 15,000 temples in Japan, and "Rinzai," from the "Lin-Chi" sect in China, with about 7,000 temples in Japan.

In the West, readers have been more readily exposed to the teachings of Rinzai, the somewhat smaller sect, because of the popularity of Daisetz Suzuki's writings; he chose to concentrate on Rinzai and the Koan teaching, and his works have been well-received in western countries. Had he chosen to translate the "Shobogenzo," the great work of Soto's founder, Dogen Zenji, and expound Zen from the Soto standpoint, our orientation in the West might have been quite different. However, it is best to remember that the Teacher Dogen, probably Japan's greatest philosopher, as well as its premier Soto Zen figure, did not use the term "Soto Zen" at all. Moreover, he did not like the word "Zen," since it was divisive. He saw himself as a "Buddhist," one who had received the main line "Transmission of Mind" while in China, and saw no reason to propagate sects, as such, within the tradition of Buddhism or the meditation branch, Zen.

There is a third school in Japan, the Obaku sect, named after Rinzai's teacher. It is barely hanging on, however, and may eventually expire. This sect, which was not one of the five great Chinese divisions of Zen, uses the Nembutsu of Shin Buddhism and has been influenced by native Shinto practices. It is hardly likely that a visitor to Japan will be exposed to the Obaku influence, so it is best to concentrate on the two great schools, Rinzai and Soto.

For the beginner who is not interested in the difference between the teachings of the sects, it is perhaps best to think of Zen as Zen, with no differentiation whatever. Unless one is going to Japan to receive special instruction or is sitting at one of the zendos in the United States which have as their masters those who have received Inka (complete approval by *their* masters) in one or the other of the sects, it would be best for the Zen meditator to *follow instructions without regard to differences* in sects.

Once the beginner has taken his or her seat, as instructed in the previous chapter, that person must now begin to face his

or her thoughts.   I always emphasize that the experienced
meditator is like a carpenter. One goes to work deliberately and
with great purpose, not wandering around in a sea of confusing
thoughts or thinking of some ephemeral "spirituality." The first
thing the beginning sitter should do is *count breaths*. Without
altering the breathing in any way, the meditator should count
either the inbreaths or the outbreaths, not both. It is important
that the eyes are kept open, as such counting of the breaths can
lead to a deep state of trance if the eyes are closed. The Buddha
suggested such counting with eyes closed as the way to the
"Dhyana Absorption," but this is not what we are aiming at in
Zen practice; such absorptions are the deep meditative states of
orthodox Buddhism.

Buddhism does not believe in breath control and
pranayamic exercises, so the breath is not held and it is not
interfered with. Actually, we are working with a mind-body
continuum in Zen, and Yogic practices of breath control, however
advantageous, have no part in this practice. Just count the
inbreaths or outbreaths, not both. It may be easier to count to
twenty, then start over. The meditator, without looking, will be
aware of the rising and falling of the abdomen and chest. In a
sense, he or she is "being breathed." The beginner should make
no effort to influence this great activity, but should simply count.

As one becomes more used to the breath, the meditator
may leave off counting the breaths and merely watch them. He
or she notes if the breath is long or short and if it is coarse or
fine. Watching the breath, the mind is occupied; there is no
room for extraneous thinking (which, nevertheless, will arise).

This "watching the breath" is one of the four great
awarenesses of the Buddha's Satipatthana Meditation and is one
of the greatest aids to Zen practice. It is also a way of quieting
the mind, affording great equanimity and bringing the physical
being into balance. In his "Yasenkanna," Hakuin Zenji tells how,
when he reached the mountain cave of the Great Hermit, Hakuyu,

he rested on a large rock and proceeded to count his breath up into the thousands before venturing into the cave. If one, at the time of great anger or trepidation, will pause to count the breath in this manner, he or she will find that it greatly helps his or her state of mind. A calm mind brings an unlabored breath and a disturbed mind, as in times of fear, causes an uneven and coarse breath. So we can work from either side. By calming the mind, the breath is mastered. By watching the breath, the mind is calmed.

In time, the meditator will begin to realize that a "single breath has extension in time, possessing a beginning, a middle and an end. The beginning of each new breath will become apparent. After long practice, experience of some mental image, such as a bluish mass or star (not some psychic vision) will show true absorption and one-pointedness."

We must not only observe the physical process but also the mental process that notes it — hence the following:

Another way to occupy the mind is to watch the thinking process. The thoughts come and go, and we watch them quietly without attempting to interfere with them. Although some have instructed that we should cut off each thought as it arises, to bring the mind to a thoughtless condition, this is not true Zen practice. We watch the thoughts but do not interfere with them and do not identify with them. Something is thinking. The ancient Japanese Zen Teacher, Basui, instructed a dying monk to "just find the essence of this mind." When we watch the thinking process, we are working toward that end.

We do not ask where the thoughts come from and where they are going, what they mean, or if they are "good" or "bad." We simply watch the thinking process itself. It is not easy to keep such concentration, and the mind will tend to wander. As soon as we realize it has wandered away, we bring it back to the object of concentration.

"I am tending an ox," stated the monk to the Master. "How do you tend an ox?" asked the latter. "When he wanders off to other fields, I ruthlessly drag him back by the nose!" was the answer. This is descriptive of our work in bringing the wandering mind back to observing the thinking process.

While the mind does tend to wander, it is important that we do not follow idle thoughts down alleys and byways. Daydreaming can be pleasant, and it may be the first instinct to follow what is pleasant. However, we must drag the ox back and ruthlessly cut off all wandering as soon as we are aware of it. In time, the mind will tend to stay with the object of concentration (in this case, watching the thinking process) and not wander off very often.

In Soto Zen, we place the concentration on the left hand, that is, at the spot just below the navel. This is our thought, and no other is needed. Such concentration must not be too intense, or it will bring about physiological changes in the fire of the digestive tract. Diarrhea is then a possibility. When we concentrate on the spot below the navel, our thought has entered a channel that extends upward through the hara and the nose to the "Hall of Jade," the spot just above and between the eyes, often referred to as the "third eye" in occult literature. Sometimes I have instructed T'ai Chi students to place their concentration in the soles of the feet (the "bubbling spring") or on the big toe, both of which are connected to the central meridian that runs up the front of the body.

The Rinzai Zen student will probably have a Koan on which to meditate. (This does not mean to constantly ruminate on it and worry it, mentally, from every angle.) This Koan, given by a Master, must be passed or solved to the satisfaction of the teacher. Those who have had true Koan practice know that a physical change seems to occur whenever one has been able to solve the Koan. It is a great moment. Actually, it is not unusual for a true Zen student or a monk to grapple with one Koan for five years or more before reaching the end of the road.

Accordingly, it would be useful to comment a bit on the Koan exercise, without attempting to go into great detail (there are some good books on Koan practice, but study of these books can actually be detrimental in the work with the Koan, which is highly individual — there are no "right" and "wrong" answers!).

"Koan" is the Japanese pronunciation for the Chinese "kung-an," which literally means a "case." At some time in the past, there has been an historical encounter between monk and Master, or two Masters, and the dialogue (Mondo) that has come from this meeting is the "case" involved. To be a true Koan, it must have the potentiality of shocking one into enlightenment. It is not just an aimless existential question invented by someone. I mention this because there are some who have had no Zen training who make up problems, such as "Where does the wind come from?" and pass them along to the gullible as "Koans." This is a mockery of Zen training and transmission.

The word "Koan" actually refers to the whole exchange, not just the word or words given by the Master to the student. The Chinese have an expression, "H'ua T'ou," which refers to the part on which the student will actually meditate. However, today, in Japan and elsewhere, the word "Koan" is used to denote the problem on which the student (sitter) will ponder. This means, if the meditator is doing true Koan practice, that he or she will carry the Koan with him or her at all times, not only when "sitting." For this reason, it is my opinion that the true Koan practice is possible only for monks or specially motivated meditators. For the casual sitter to drop the Koan when he or she leaves the Zendo and pick it up again when returning to Zen sitting is not compatible with carrying successful practice through to the desired end. In the West, where there are few Zen monks, we find this happening. The teacher gives a Koan problem to a sitter, sometimes when the student has had no indoctrination in what the Koan is and what he or she is to do with it, and the latter takes it up and puts it down as the mood prevails. This is not Koan practice and is doomed to failure.

A Japanese Master came upon his lay student, who was attempting to place coins upon a string. So strong was the student's concentration on his Koan that he was unable to carry out this simple task! "When concentration reaches such a stage, we do not have to worry about the eventual success of the practice!" commented the teacher. Such perseverance is rare these days.

The sitter soon learns that it is not possible to "solve" the Koan by intellectual effort. Beginning his or her spell of sitting, the meditator will attain a level of concentration and then "drop in" his or her Koan so that it may sink into the subconscious mind and grow as the "I Chin(g)" or great doubt that is needed for successful Koan practice. For those willing to make exceptional effort, the seven-day meditation known as "Dai Sesshin" is the best possible time at which to make progress in Koan practice, perhaps even to the point of fruition. Sometimes Zendos in Japan and America have one-day or two-day Sesshin, and these are quite rigorous. For the seven-day meditation, the aspirant brings a sleeping bag or some other vehicle in which to catch a few hours of sleep. He or she spends the entire week at the Zendo, and this is the one time the Zen person does no physical labor. At some Shesshin, no bathing is allowed; all concentration is on Zazen. From the time the sitter arises in the morning (usually at about 3:00 a.m.) until he or she goes to sleep at night, that person will do periods of intense Zazen, interspersed with as many as four visits a day to the Master in Sanzen. Fortunate is the aspirant who can have such intimate contact with a Zen Master, and such repeated opportunity to work with one's Koan under ideal circumstances.

It is assumed that anybody undertaking such a rigorous schedule — the seven days of sitting in Dai Sesshin — is not a casual practitioner. There will be pain in the legs from continued sitting. According to one master, this will reach its peak between the third and fourth days, after which the sitter will "begin to catch the rhythm of Sesshin." There will be little sleep, and not much is needed when one is doing so much meditation. The food at Dai Sesshin is always more substantial and usually better-tasting (while still being vegetarian) than is usually the case at a temple or Zendo. The one practicing is making a great effort, and it is felt that good food, if not heavy, will help that effort. Frequent interludes of drinking tea are inserted into the sitting periods, not for social reasons, but because the flow of Prana (Chi, Ki) that will occur in good sitting tends to dry the fluids of the body and makes the throat parched and thirsty.

One should not attempt such an undertaking until one has become an experienced sitter. Such prolonged sitting can be hazardous to a beginner. There is the case of a renowned British scholar who went to the Orient and, without any previous experience in Zen sitting, attempted to do the whole Dai Sesshin. This courageous but foolhardy effort resulted in a stretching of the tendons that permanently disabled the man. It is said that he only partially recovered from this experience, and he never sat Zazen again.

It is better if one does what one can and does not attempt heroic tasks. It is the steady, continued effort in Zen Meditation that gets results. Such effort is cumulative, even though it is well-known that the actual Enlightenment experience is sudden and instantaneous, with no degrees. Sudden Enlightenment is the result of long and continued practice.

The reader, who may be about to attempt Zen Meditation for the first time may, nevertheless, be curious about Koan practice, about which he or she may have heard much. Accordingly, I am going to mention a few well-known Koans on which the meditator may wish to work.

A good beginning Koan problem is, "Who hears the Buddha's voice?" In time, the aspirant may come up with a reasonable answer, such as "When one is Buddha, one hears Buddha's voice," or "It is Buddha who hears Buddha's voice." However, to present such an answer to a Master in Sanzen, the meditator will have to convince the Master that his or her understanding goes beyond the intellectual. Of course, this Koan points at the Buddha Nature that is within all of us and is the essence of all sentient beings.

Since the Buddha Nature is present in all, how do we explain Chao Chou's (Joshu's) answer to the monk who asked him if a dog has Buddha Nature? The Master simply answered, "Wu" (Mu in Japanese), and the word "Wu" in Chinese, depending on the tone level used, can mean "negation" or "no." It is my understanding that the word "Wu" was not used as "no" but as the Chinese equivalent of Sunya or Sunyata, the great Emptiness (Void) in Sanskrit. In other words, I feel the Master was answering the question by pointing to the void, in which all things exist. However, that is my personal solution of the Koan and will not do for another meditator. If you are going to take this "Wu" (or "Mu") as your Koan, you must wrestle with it yourself and come up with your own solution. Since it is well-known that all sentient beings have Buddha Nature, why did Chao Chou answer in this way? "Wu" (or Mu) is not to be treated as a Mantra, endlessly to be repeated. Dropped into the subconscious, it should eventually produce surprising results if one is sincere about one's practice.

Other well-known Koans are the following, any one of which may be suitable for the serious sitter:

"You have heard the sound of two hands clapping. Now, what is the sound of one hand?" It is obvious that one hand does not make any sound, so this soundless sound must be your real self. Can you manifest this one hand sound? If one is stuck with literal thinking, that person will not solve such a Koan in a million years.

And if one does solve it to a teacher's satisfaction, he or she may then have to grapple with "How big is One Hand Sound?" This can be a follow-up Koan to the previous one when the former is resolved to the teacher's satisfaction.

Such Koans as "Dry Dung" and "Cypress Tree in the Garden," which represent illogical answers to monks' questions, are too difficult for beginners to contend with. If the aspirant will stick to the facts of existence and think only in terms of the "now," it may help in work with the Koan.

There are many levels of Koans. It may be easy for a beginner to intellectually comprehend Hui-neng's instructions to his first student (who may have come to kill him!): "Thinking of neither good nor evil, at this exact moment what is your Original Face?" This is equivalent to saying, before your parents conceived you, what were you, and it also points at the mind without distinctions, which is the mind in its natural and enlightened state.

Also fairly simple is, "If the many return to the One, to what does the One return?" While simple to understand in its word form, the "meaning," if we can talk about a "meaning" in connection with a Koan, is far from simple.

If the prospective meditator is attracted by Koan practice, he or she can use one of the above examples as a Koan. "Wu" is a particularly appropriate vehicle as it has no semantic meaning to a Westerner, and there is little to grasp. If one will imagine having fallen into a deserted well, and a thin clothesline known as "wu" extends down the side of the well, enabling him or her to grasp the line and slowly and painfully being able to walk up the sides of the well, he or she will get the idea. Since that person's life depends on hanging on to this single thread, he or she will not, no matter how painful it becomes, let go of the line until he or she has used it to climb to the top of the well and

has escaped from his or her threatened tomb. One must hang on
to one's Koan with just this determination. Masters tell us that,
if one does, the mind's own illumination will certainly burst into
brightness and the matter will be solved for all time — he or she
will be out of the well!

Chapter 4
LOSING OURSELVES
(we find ourselves)

I will continue to deal with the mental practices of Zen, the discipline of the mind that will be pursued once the meditator has taken his or her seat for Zazen. Of course, the number and variety of methods is not important. The idea is not to offer a smorgasbord so that the sitter can amuse him or herself by going from one technique to another. However, I am speaking to the prospective sitter as a do-it-yourself meditator who must find a way suitable to him or herself and one that is compatible with the sitter's nature. Accordingly, I want to make available a few methods of concentration that may greatly help the beginning Zen practice.

When Zen monks first began to appear in Japan, they usually stayed at Tendai Buddhist temples, such as the famous one on the top of Mount Hiei near Kyoto. Tendai is the Japanese branch of the Chinese T'ien-t'ai, which had always had a strong affinity with Ch'an and Zen followers. Accordingly, it is not strange that Zen people often use the deceptively simple T'ien-t'ai meditation known as Chih-Kuan (Shi Kan in Japanese). The Buddha himself had often spoken of this method as Samatha-Samapatti (sometimes referred to, mistakenly, as Samatha-Vipassana), and the "Surangama Sutra" has an exhaustive study of the different ways of combining these with Dhyana (meditation or absorption).   Chih-Kuan can literally mean "stopping" and "a view."

The Chinese believe the most effective meditation begins with fixation.   That is, after being seated, one places one's concentration on some place in the body, such as the tip of the nose, the spot between the eyes, or the T'an T'ien two inches below the navel.   The effects will be slightly different according to which of these three is used, even though they are connected by the central meridian channel.   Sometimes meditators have shifted their concentration from one spot to another after keeping it in the same place for a long while.   Simply stated, "Chih" consists of anchoring the mind to one place through such fixation.   Then, as long as the meditation goes along smoothly, one continues with the concentration on the chosen spot (Shikan-taza, with the thought focused on the left hand below the navel, is essentially the same thing).   However, after a while, extraneous thoughts begin to arise.   When their number and frequency become great, one turns from the fixation to watch the thoughts, noting where they arise and where they are going.   Such close observation will cause the thoughts to disappear, and then one returns to the fixation, concentrating on the spot chosen.

This relatively simple two-part activity will enable the meditator to fully concentrate, and eventually the light of the Unconditioned Mind will shine through.   There are many variations on this pattern; however, it will be best for any except the most experienced meditators to work with the "Chih" and the "Kuan" alone — these are sufficient for the long road to Enlightenment, and many Chinese monks, in ancient days, found them effective.

When I sat meditation for the first time with a Chinese Master, he varied this routine a bit. He instructed me to open my eyes and fasten my gaze on a spot in the wall.   Then he instructed me to close my eyes but to keep watching the same spot in memory.   Soon a strong psychic experience occurred. Not believing it at first, I opened my eyes and then repeated the process. Again, the same experience, usually called "Makyo" in Japanese Zen, occurred. At that moment the interpreter commanded, "Tell the teacher your experience!" Feeling that the Master had deliberately caused this psychic happening in order to show off, I did not mention it at the time. Once again the interpreter said, "Tell the teacher your experience!" I did not do so, feeling it was only meant to impress the others present. Later, on a boat back to America, in re-reading the Taoist classic, *Secret of the Golden Flower*, I came across the same exact experience, and then proceeded to write a letter to the teacher, telling him of it. So it is apparent that this method of memorizing a spot on the wall and then gazing at it with eyes closed can have effect. One may even wish to shift the memorized spot to the place between the eyes (in which case a slowly-swelling blue mass may be observed) or to the place below the navel. However, this takes an effort in visualization and is really more in keeping with Tibetan Buddhism than Zen itself.

The physical manifestations resulting from such concentration are, in themselves, important, but under no circumstances should they be clung to. Ch'an is often called "A Study of Mind," and such experiences are, themselves, creations of the mind, no matter how satisfying they may seem. There are physical changes that take place in true Zen practice, and one who does not realize this does not understand the true Zen path. Buddhism does not deal with a transcendental God, off somewhere apart from our world. In true Buddhist practice, Samsara (the world of phenomena) is Nirvana (the Absolute or Blissful Unconditioned), and it is right here in the body that Enlightenment must be experienced. In this way Zen practice greatly differs from the traditional Samkya Yoga paths of India where there is a duality between the Purity of the Absolute and the Soiled Trash of the world. Indian thought speaks of Maya, the world of illusion, but Zen says that right in the midst of this illusion, right in the heart of the passions, is Reality.

A somewhat more esoteric method of concentration, and one that will have strong physical effects, is described by Hakuin in his "Yasenkanna." It seems to have almost disappeared in Japan, though in the past, such monks as the famous Ryokan wrote that it greatly aided them in their Zen practice. Hakuin called it "Nai Kan" (Inner Concentration or Inner Efficiency), and he learned it from the hermit Hakuyu, who admitted it was Taoist in origin. It is called "Nei Kung"* in Chinese, and is one of the favored "Chi Kung" practices in that country — that is, a favorable way to circulate the Life Energy (Vital Force) known as Chi, corresponding to the Indian Prana.

This method can be practiced as a meditation during Zazen sitting, or it can be done lying flat on the back before one goes to sleep at night. If the latter is used, the meditator puts his or her legs together, closes the eyes, and continually repeats the following four affirmations:

1) This Energy Sea, this Tanden, from below the navel to the soles of the feet, full of my Original Face: where are the nostrils on this Face?

2) This Energy Sea, this Tanden, from below the navel to the soles of the feet, full of my True Home: No need of a message from this Home.

3) This Energy Sea, this Tanden, from below the navel to the soles of the feet, full of the Pure Land of Consciousness only: what need of outer pomp for this Pure Land?

---

*For a more detailed account of this and other so-called "healing" forms of meditation, the reader may wish to consult Justin Stone's *Meditation for Healing*, where the affirmations listed are treated in Chapter 4, the section on Nei Kung.

4) This Energy Sea, this Tanden, from below the navel to the soles of the feet, full of the Amida Buddha of heart and body: what Dharma would this Amida be preaching?

The meditator can also, if so minded, insert the phrase "This flowing, healing Chi" along with the affirmations, in any spot he or she deems acceptable, particularly if that person wishes to develop a healing heat current.

It will be noted that terms from other schools of Buddhism are being used in this meditation. The "Pure Land" refers to the Western Paradise of Shin Buddhism, and Amida Buddha is the Buddha of Infinite Light, known as "Amitabha" in India and China. Zen knows of no reason why it shouldn't use any expedients at all on the path to Enlightenment. Any sectarian feelings would be decidedly detrimental. Zen is a way of being free from all conditions while in the midst of conditions.

If this meditation is practiced at night, one may awaken from sleep and feel a surge of heat pouring through the body. This will carry a good deal of energy with it, and it is felt to be healing in nature. The meditator can practice this discipline at night before going to bed — lying flat on the back with eyes closed and legs pressed together — or while sitting Zazen, but not both. Almost certainly one will fall asleep while doing it at night, with eyes closed, and Hakuin felt this was helpful, usually leading to a sound and revivifying sleep. If one then practices it while sitting in Zazen posture, the meditator may become drowsy, limiting the effectiveness of his or her sitting.

Chanting is common to most religions, and it is a particularly powerful practice when performed by a group. It is easy to lose oneself in the volume of sound when there are others chanting at the same time, and there are no gaps when one pauses for breath. It doesn't matter whether the chanting is in

Latin, in Sanskrit, or in Chinese-Japanese — all three languages lend themselves to such activity. Today there is a good deal of controversy over the question of chanting in English, much as there is over the modern trend toward singing opera in English, regardless of whether the original language was Italian, French, or German.

Those in favor of chanting Buddhist Sutras in English feel it is a help for the chanter to know what he or she is chanting. Since there is nothing sacred about the Chinese and Japanese languages and since most Sutras in those languages originally were translated from Sanskrit or Pali, or worse, were trans-literated from those languages, the proponents of English chanting see no reason why the Sutras shouldn't be translated again and chanted in the chanters' own tongue.

On the other hand, traditional Japanese and Chinese Masters are usually very strongly against such practice. They are used to hearing the Sutras in the short sounds of Chinese and do not feel they sound right in English. Moreover, they do not feel it is important for the chanter to attach semantic meaning to what is being chanted. Just as a Mantra is a sound beyond ordinary meaning, so they feel chanting of the sounds in the Sutras is sufficient. Again, the chanter can, if he or she wishes, study the meaning of the sutra from other translated sources, while continuing to chant the traditional way.

Whether the reader decides to chant with a group, which is to be desired — particularly if it can be done with ceremony in a temple or zendo — or gets in the habit of chanting once or twice a day alone, I do want to recommend the practice. After finishing the amount of meditation the sitter has pre-decided, he or she might wish to chant the relatively short "Heart Sutra" ("Hridaya" in Sanskrit and "Maka Hanya Haramita Shin Gyo" in the Chinese transliteration), following which one should make three bows all the way to the floor. These bows do not mean paying reverence to anything or anyone, though they may be made in the direction of a Buddha figure. They do encourage humility and thanksgiving, which are helpful in spiritual practice. Following is the "Heart Sutra" in both Chinese-Japanese and in English translation. By "Heart" is meant the Heart of the Prajna-paramita; that is, the gist of the over 1600 Sutras of the Prajna-paramita group. Almost all true Buddhism is contained in this little gem and after chanting it daily in the Chinese-Japanese sounds, the practitioner will do well to study the English translation carefully.

MAKA HANYA HARAMITA SHIN GYO
Kan-Ji-zai Bo-sa gyo jin Han-nya Ha-ra-mi-ta ji
Sho-ken go un kai ku do is-sai ku-yaku
Sha-ri-shi shiki fu i ku ku
Fu i shiki shiki soku ze ku ku
Soku ze shiki ju so gyo shiki yaku-bu nyo ze
Sha-ri-shi ze sho-ho ku-so fu sho fu metsu
Fu ku fu jo fu zo fu gen
Ze-ko ku chu mu shiki mu ju so gyo shiki
Mu gen ni bi zets shin ni mu shiki sho ko mi
Soku ho mu gen kai nai-shi
Mu i-shiki-kai mu mu-myo yaku
Mu mu-myo jin nai-shi
Mu ro shi yaku mu ro shi jin
Mu ku shu metsu do
Mu chi yaku mu toku i
Mu sho to Ko Bo-dai-sat-ta e
Han-nya Ha-ra-mi-ta ko shin
Mu ke-ge mu-ke-ge ko
Mu u ku-fu on-ri is-sai
Ten-do mu so ku-gyo Ne-han
San-ze sho Butsu e
Han-nya Ha-ra-mi-ta ko

Toku a noku ta ra san myaku san bo dai
Ko Chi Han-nya Ha-ra-mi-ta ze
Dai shin shu ze dai myo shu ze
Mu-jo-shu ze mu-to-do shu no jo
Is-sai ku shin-jitsu fu ko ko setsu
Han-nya Ha-ra-mi-ta shu
Soku setsu shu watsu
GYA-TE GYA-TE HA-RA GYA-TE
HA-RA-SO GYA-TE BO-DHI SOWA-KA
HAN-NYA SHIN-GYO.

(The last three lines, in capital letters, are the "unsurpassed" Mantra spoken by Kan-Ji-Zai — Avalokitesvara in Indian tongues — and is transliterated from the original GATE GATE PARAGATE PARASAMGATE BODHI SVAHA. While a mantra should never be changed, the Chinese found it impossible to pronounce the Sanskrit syllables and did the transliteration.)

HEART (HRIDAYA) SUTRA
(translated into English)

When Bodhisattva Avalokitesvara practiced the profound Prajna-paramita, he investigated and perceived that the five aggregates (Skandhas) were non-existent, thus securing this deliverance from all distress and suffering.

Sariputra! Form does not differ from the Void, nor the Void from Form. Form is identical with Void and Void is identical with Form. So also with Perception, Consciousness, Feeling, and Knowledge in relation to the Void.

Sariputra! The Void, of all things, is not created, not annihilated, not impure, not pure, not increasing, and not decreasing.

Therefore, with the Void, there is no form, no perception, no consciousness, no feeling, and no knowledge. There is no eye, ear, nose, tongue, body, and mind; there is no form, sound, smell, taste, touch, and idea. There are no such things as the eighteen realms of sense, from the realm of sight up to that of the faculty of mind; there are no such things as the twelve links in the chain of existence from ignorance and the ending of ignorance up to old age and death, with, also, the ending of old age and death; there are no such things as the Four Noble Truths and there is no Wisdom and no gain.

Because of gainlessness, Bodhisattvas, who rely on Prajna-paramita, have no hindrance in their hearts, and since they have no hindrance, they have no fear, are free from contrary and delusive ideas, and attain the final Nirvana.

All the Buddhas of the past, present, and future obtain complete vision and perfect Enlightenment by relying on Prajna-paramita. So we know that Prajna-paramita is the great supernatural Mantra, the great bright, unsurpassed, and unequalled Mantra, which can truly and without fail wipe out all suffering.

Therefore, he uttered the Prajna-paramita Mantra, which reads:

GATE, GATE, PARAGATE, PARASAMGATE, BODHI SVAHA!

(The above based on the translation, with minor correction, from the original Sanskrit by Tripitaka-Master Hsuen-tsang of the Tang Dynasty. Translated from Chinese into English by Upsaka Lu K'uan-yu and given out by the American Academy of Chinese Culture in Los Angeles.)

Zen is a branch of Mahayana Buddhism and, as such, the ideal is the Bodhisattva, who vows to save all sentient beings. The Buddha was a Bodhisattva before attaining Buddhahood. Therefore, in full knowledge of what he or she is doing, the meditator, after finishing the chanting of the Sutra, might wish to chant "The Four Vows," which follow in Chinese-Japanese and in English translation; he or she will follow these with the three deep bows. Certainly, if one is a practising Buddhist, he or she

will want to take these vows, and it is customary to finish most
Zen Meditation sessions with the chanting of the vows.

THE FOUR VOWS

(to be repeated three times)

SHU JO MU HEN SEI GAN DO
BON NO MU JIN SEI GAN DAN
HO MON MU RYO SEI GAN GAKU
BUTSU DO MU JO SEI GAN JO

It is suggested that the above be chanted from deep down
in the stomach, or even the Tanden, as if one were swallowing
the words.

THE FOUR VOWS IN ENGLISH TRANSLATION

Sentient beings are numberless;
I take a vow to save them all.
The deluding passions are inexhaustible;
I take a vow to destroy them all.
The gates of the Law (Dharma) are countless;
I vow to enter every one.
The Buddha Way is supreme;
I take a vow to fulfill it.

In regard to chanting and reading the "Heart Sutra"
above, it should be remembered that Zen Masters have said, "A
deluded mind is moved by the Sutras; an enlightened mind
moves the Sutras. Eventually the Sutras move the Sutras."

In teaching T'ai Chi Ch'uan and T'ai Chi Chih, I have
often pointed out to students that a really joyous moment is one
when, suddenly, no one is doing T'ai Chi. The former Do-er is
now just observing and, truthfully, T'ai Chi is doing T'ai Chi.
The preceding comments have the same meaning. Chanting
should be performed with this aim in mind, to eliminate the

chanter and just let there be chanting. If one can chant from the depths of the diaphragm and with the whole heart and body, without emphasizing individual words or sounds, he or she will feel an overpowering rhythm that has a life of its own, and there will be a steady flow of deep sound from this serious practice, engulfing the chanter and causing that person to die the great Zen Death.

Chapter 5
WITHOUT SUBJECT, WITHOUT OBJECT
(where are we?)

In this chapter I am going to present two other valid modes of meditation for Zen students. Generally, those who have practiced in the West will not be aware of these because the teaching they have received has all been Japanese-influenced. Most of what has been read has been written by Japanese authors, such as D.T. Suzuki, or by westerners who have read Suzuki and synthesized, in their own books, what he has said. Consequently, knowledge of Chinese Ch'an has not been disseminated to the same extent as that of Japanese Zen. Of the two modes I will present, one was used in China and the other is from pre-Zen India.

Lin-Chi I-hsuan lived in the ninth century in China and, as is well-known, was the favorite student and successor of Huang-po (Obaku in Japanese), though, oddly enough, he experienced his Enlightenment with another Master. A quiet, introverted, and pietistic monk, Lin-Chi became a roaring lion upon his Enlightenment, proceeding to slap the face of his Master, Huang-po, when he (Lin-Chi) had returned to see the latter immediately after his great experience. This caused the teacher to exclaim, "So you have come to beard the lion in his own den!" Undoubtedly, Huang-po was delighted with this and subsequent acts of independence on the part of the man he knew was to be his successor. Zen "Samu" means that Master and pupils work together in equality, expressing their Buddha nature in every activity, no matter how mundane. It is a far different relationship from that of disciple (Chela) and Guru in India, where such things as "Guru Worship Day" exist. If the Zen student were to worship the teacher, or even the Buddha, he or she would probably be struck and even kicked to the ground by the iconoclastic Master. The purpose of Zen training is to free one, not to bind one. The teacher searches for one who does not want to be deluded, even by the teacher himself.

Few other Zen Masters have contributed as much to the overall Zen picture as has Lin-Chi, who was later known as Rinzai in Japan. His sect of Zen became the dominant one in China in later years, overshadowing, and even assimilating, others of the Big Five. Lin-Chi himself became known for his shouts, using them in various ways to prod disciples into seeing their own nature. He defined some of these as "shouts not used as shouts," and a familiar saying in China was "Te-shan for his blows, Lin-Chi for his shouts." Te-shan was a contemporary Zen teacher, well-known for his strict disciplinary actions.

Because of Lin-Chi's influence and because, as Rinzai, he later had such an effect on Japanese Zen (Rinzai Zen first came to Japan in the second half of the twelfth century, brought by the great Eisai, who was also the importer of the Tea Ceremony — "Cha No Yu" — that has played such an important role in Japanese life), it is hard to understand why his profound teaching of the four uses of subject and object have not been taught in Japanese Zen circles.

There are many ways this teaching can be used, and I am going to offer it here as a means of four-part meditation, leading the meditator to the inevitable ending, experience of the vast Void.

First, the sitter concentrates on the OBJECT ONLY, eliminating all thought of the subject. This pure objectivity means sinking entirely into the object of concentration, giving up oneself completely. I remember one time when it was arranged for a Zen Roshi to attend a concert by a famous Indian musician, a master of the sitar. Roshi took along ten students, and really enjoyed the evening. Afterward, he remonstrated with them, saying they did not fully engross themselves in the music. "I really got inside the music!" he declared, pointing out that others tend to drift off and think about their problems, day-dream, etc. This is why the Zen adept feels he or she is saying something unusual in remarking, "When I eat, I eat; and when I sleep, I sleep." The ability to sink into the object and lose ourselves is an important one. When we see the flying birds, we are the flying birds — we have died to ourselves and nothing is left over. In this way we unify all things. So Lin-Chi said, "Eliminate the subject and rest in the object only."

Next, the sitter shifts concentration to the subject, the one who is doing the observing. Completely eliminating the object, one concentrates on the SUBJECT ONLY. This is not easy to do.

The third step occurs when the sitter concentrates on BOTH THE SUBJECT AND THE OBJECT. Now he or she has broadened the scope of the meditation and becomes aware of the polarity of existence, the two poles. This, of course, is ancient Chinese teaching, the Doctrine of the Mean. The Sixth Patriarch instructed his disciples to always speak in terms of the opposites; that is, when greatness was mentioned, to answer in terms of smallness, to counter talk of "good" with something about "bad." In this way, the Mean is pointed to, something that is at neither end of the polarity, that is not conditioned, and that, therefore, represents Reality. This is also the teaching of the Middle Way in Buddhism. Thus, at this stage, we concentrate on the concentrator *and* on the thing concentrated upon — both the subject and the object.

Finally, in the fourth step, we ELIMINATE BOTH THE SUBJECT AND THE OBJECT and just meditate.   After proceeding through the other three steps, this should not be hard to do. Such abstract meditation can bring an overwhelming sense of emptiness — which might be experienced as "fullness" by one trained in a different tradition — and will allow the meditator to rest easily in the "unconditioned."

When I have taught the Great Circle Meditation* to students, I have found that, after going through all the preliminaries and bringing the great light (i.e. the "proper thought") back to the spot below the navel, it is very easy for them to sit in abstract meditation for long periods of time. One student, being questioned as to what he found at that point, simply replied that, "It was awfully empty!"

These four steps, in which we progressively think of the object, then the subject, the subject and the object, and finally, eliminating both subject and object, or No Thing, can be done separately or all at one sitting. A serious meditator may want to take only step one in his or her next meditation period, then proceed to the subsequent steps in following periods. If it is done in separate steps, in this way, it is suggested that eventually, the meditator run through all four familiar stages consecutively at one sitting after having become well-grounded in the separate steps.

Do not let some well-meaning friend, or even a monk with limited view, talk you out of trying this meditation simply because that person is not familiar with it and his or her Master did not teach it! It is a product of Rinzai's teaching and, as such, very valid.

---

*The Great Circle Meditation is taught in the author's book *T'ai Chi Chih/Joy thru Movement.*

The Satipatthana Meditation has often been called "The Way of Mindfulness," and was the meditative process that Gautama himself used on his way to becoming the Buddha. Countless Sutras (Buddhist Scriptures) describe the value of this Way of Mindfulness, usually beginning with, "Herein dwells the monk, mindfully contemplating —," and then follows a description of the object of contemplation. It is customary for Zen people to say that, "Buddha reached his Enlightenment through Zen," but they do not say what that Zen consisted of. It could not have been Koan training because that began over a thousand years later in China. While Zen traces its lineage all the way back to the Buddha, in a sense making him the First Zen Patriarch, there is no doubt that Chinese Ch'an became much different from the original teachings of the Perfect One, the teachings more apt to be found in Theravada Buddhist Centers today than in such Mahayana Buddhist places as Zen temples.

I do believe, however, that Zen development owed much to the Satipatthana Meditation. Zen stresses "twenty-four-hour awareness," and this is exactly what the Satipatthana tends to bring about. Developments of this meditation have been many, and offshoots have become particularly popular in Burma, where the highly-concentrated Burmese Method is taught. Instruction in this method may also be found in Ceylon (Sri Lanka) and parts of India today. These developments, however, are not compatible with Zen practice, while the original four subjects of Satipatthana Meditation fit very well into the Zen scheme of things. I am simply going to give the four progressive subjects of meditation, without elaborating on them. One could write volumes on each one, if so desired, but then we would be getting over into the field of philosophy, and the main purpose of this book is instruction in Zen Buddhist Meditation.

As with the Lin-Chi four subjects of meditation, these four "Ways of Mindfulness" may be contemplated at one sitting or individually, over a period of many sittings. The Satipatthana

is not a casual meditation. One does not pick it up for a few
minutes a day, as with the repetition of a Mantra in forms of
Indian Japa, and then drop it again. It is a way to the Highest
and should be treated with great respect.

The SATIPATTHANA:

First, we become aware of the BODY through the
breathing process. The Zen student will already be familiar with
a similar step, previously described. Watching — or literally
being aware of — the rise and fall of the diaphragm, we observe
the breathing. As noted, if it is a long breath, so be it; we are
aware that we are breathing a long breath. If a short breath, we
do not try to change it — we are aware that we are breathing a
short breath. In the beginning it will not be easy for the
meditator to breathe naturally, and there may be a tendency to
rush the breath. In time this will smooth out.

If this first step is carried over into everyday living, the
meditator will be conscious that one is walking, that one is
standing, that one is sitting, or that one is lying down. At all
times he or she will be aware of these four basic attitudes.
Strangely enough, the Buddha's cousin and loyal attendant,
Ananda, experienced Enlightenment in the period *between* two of
these states. It was while in the act of lying down, when he was
no longer standing and not yet lying down, that he reached the
end of the long road he had pursued so assiduously.

In the second meditation, the sitter contemplates the
FEELINGS. Some teachers point out that this means the feelings
before emotion. The sitter simply becomes aware of all feelings,
internal and external, noting that, "This is a pleasant feeling, this
is a painful feeling, this is a neutral feeling with no classification
at all." The same would be true of all perceptions or sensations.
If it is an inner feeling, it may be of a worldly nature, or it may
be what the meditator thinks of as a "holy," other-worldly
feeling. An outer feeling will be some sort of touch response

(sensation of touching the pillow, feeling the breeze on the skin, etc.) that may be pleasant, unpleasant, or neutral. The sitter is simply to be aware of these feelings as they continually occur. At a more advanced stage, a meditator may wish to introspect the origination of feelings and dissolution of these feelings, not easy to detect. As one becomes more alert to them, over a period of time, the sitter will note that feelings are constantly dissolving. Indeed, all life will eventually break down into such origination and dissolution, and the serious meditator will come to the realization of Anicca, impermanence. Processes are coming and going constantly, but nothing seems permanent. This breaks down much of what we have been conditioned to believe, but the meditator must be ready to trust his or her own experience. So the contemplation of Feelings may well be the beginning of the trip to the Void, the Emptiness that so many Zen Masters insist their students taste for themselves.

The third step in the Satipatthana is the contemplation of the STATES OF MIND. The student should know the three basic states that lead to Suffering, as expounded by the Buddha — Greed, Anger, and Delusion. Lust is included with Greed and Annoyance included with Anger. Delusion is not so easy to spot, as it really means confusing the unreal with the Real, mistaking something that is only temporary with that which is permanent and without change. Carried to an extreme, almost all sense perception would have the nature of delusion, as would our ordinary view of ourselves as lasting entities when, in fact, we are the product of causes, rising when the causes come to fruition and disappearing when the effects are outworn. We must be honest enough to see clearly and not perpetuate delusive thinking in our meditation, no matter how strong such sentiment has become. It is our purpose, in this third step, to note exactly in what condition the mind is resting, without in any way attempting to judge that state. In addition to noting if the mind is with or without Greed, with or without Anger, and with or without

Delusion, it would be best for the beginner to stick with such ordinary states as "mind with anxiety," "joyous mind," "mind that is unconcerned," "impatient mind," etc., and not to worry about the more technical classifications that experienced monks may note. One should observe that mind is functioning and that the mind simply consists of thoughts. And one may also note the origination and dissolution of States of Mind at the very moment one is observing them so carefully. Such close observation of the States of Mind may tend to amaze the uninitiated at first, and it is not always easy to pinpoint the condition of the mind, which is artful in camouflage. Nevertheless, our subject of meditation is the State of Mind at this instant, and noting it accurately and without prejudice will do much to establish overall awareness.

Finally, in the fourth meditation, we will take note of MIND OBJECTS. This is different from the previous meditation, where we were determining what state the mind itself was in. Now we are being asked to note anything that comes to mind for perception — noises, thoughts, memories, wishes, sights, etc. This is by far the broadest of the four categories, and teachers say it is the one that appeals most to those with intellectual leanings. The objects of mind will come from both outside and inside. While we may seem to be deluged by such objects, the truth is that the mind can only handle one of them at a time, and the practiced mind will be able to sort them out as they occur. Again, we are asked not to make any judgment. Something is presenting itself on the screen of the mind, and we are asked to note it as it flashes there. It will dissolve and something else will appear, and we will catch that, too. This category, of course, is remarkably like regular Zen Meditation, and the student will find that such careful factual scrutinization will help with his or her Koan practice.

There are five hindrances to Enlightenment, according to Buddhist teaching. They are sense-desire, anger, laziness, worry, and doubt. The meditator is to know when a doubt is present.

Whether he or she cognizes this doubt as a mind-object or thinks of the mind as "Mind with Doubt," which would put it in the third category and not in this fourth meditation, it is helpful if one notes when these factors are present. I personally feel these five hindrances fit more easily into the third meditation, but most of the Satipatthana instructors include them with the fourth.

Experienced monks will later get into such matters as the six internal and six external sense bases (which, with the fields of sense-perception, add up to eighteen), and will note the different signs of clinging, as well as the so-called seven "factors of Enlightenment" (reality, energy, rapture, tranquility, concentration, equanimity, and mindfulness), so as to note whether they are present or absent. However, such advanced subjects of meditation are much too complex for the beginner, and it is suggested that he or she stick to successive meditations on the BODY (through the breath), the FEELINGS (inner and outer), the STATES OF MIND (concentrating particularly on Greed, Anger, and Delusion, to see if they are present or absent — that is, Mind without Greed, etc.), and the OBJECTS OF MIND (both sense perceptions and thoughts, such as memory, that present themselves to one).

These four categories, practiced faithfully, will tend to break down the very factors of consciousness. In Buddhism, consciousness is not something absolute, as it is felt to be in other Indian modes of thought. Rather, a consciousness arises when there is an object and subsides when no object presents itself. There is not one continuing consciousness, but sporadic flashes that, themselves, last for brief periods of time. This is so counter to our ordinary indoctrination that it will be necessary for us to observe without any preconceived conclusion in order to determine the truth and eventually come to the deepest insights of Buddhism. If we persist in the Satipatthana Meditation, we will certainly arrive at these deeper insights, and I see no reason why practice of the Satipatthana should not be compatible with Zen practice.

It is often pointed out that true meditation begins with "bare attention," that is, noting the present facts of existence without reacting to them and making judgments about them. One present-day non-Zen teacher of considerable influence has called this "Choiceless Awareness." The Buddha counseled:

"In what is seen, there should be only the seen; in what is heard, only the heard; in what is smelled, only that smelled; in the tasted, only that which is tasted; in what is touched, only the thing touched; with that which is thought, only the thought itself."

This is most difficult, as the mind tends to wander off into daydream and memory. Zen practice is not easy. But this is the way to True Meditation, meditation that lasts all the hours of the day.

"It is easier to give birth to one's own mother than to maintain this twenty-four hour Zen," said Master Tokuzan. The Satipatthana Meditation of Mindfulness will be of great help to the Zen practitioner in mastering the mind. When the mind is mastered, all is mastered.

Chapter 6
EMPTINESS
(emptiness, too, is empty)

One time, in Japan, two well-known Buddhists accompanied me on a visit to the house of a famous scholar, who was also considered an outstanding Zen Master. The latter was married and greeted us in the living room of his house, wearing western business clothes.

At one point in the interesting conversation, the Master took a moment to make some comments on Sunyata, the so-called Buddhist Void. "This emptiness is more real to me than the things of the world!" he declared. I was greatly surprised at this sudden dichotomy. Here were the things of the world, and over there was emptiness, and that over there was far more real than this over here.

This was not my understanding at all. The very "emptiness" *is* the multi-faceted world. If they are the same, how can we differentiate and say that is more real than this? Much more to the point is the story of the ancient Zen Master who asked a disciple, "How do you grasp the Void?"

The monk went through motions of reaching into empty space and grasping it, a logical reaction.

The Master made a gesture of impatience. "You fool!" he exclaimed, "Here is how to grasp the Void!" And so saying, he grabbed the monk's nose, twisting it and almost wrenching it off as the latter howled in pain. Here is a classic illustration of what the Buddhist Void *really* is, not something to be held up in contrast to worldly phenomena. In Buddhism, Samsara is Nirvana — the relative world is, itself, the Absolute.

I mention all this because discussion of Emptiness and Void ("Aspectlessness" is my own term) seems pertinent in this book on Zen Meditation.

When Bodhidharma advised a follower "not to have a panting heart," he was speaking of the attitude of no-attitude, awareness without distinction, the cutting off of Karma-making attachment. Just to do what must be done, without attachment to the action or the reward, is true non-attachment, not refraining from all action. Of course, this is a commentary on Karma and the fruits of Karma. In truth, it is the motive behind the action, the thought and not the movement, that matters. When we act without motive, we can meet conditions as they arise. When there is no grasping in the heart, we can respond as seems fitting, and die to each action as it is completed. We can even cut the cat in half (as Master Nansen supposedly did) and, by cutting it in half, we can unite it. The North Star can be seen in the South, and the waters of the river can be drunk with one gulp. When the heart is empty, anything is possible — but we don't act like that. We love, expecting a return, and give, anticipating a reward. This is far from Emptiness.

Chuang-tzu, the Taoist philosopher, who was much admired by Chinese Ch'an masters, spoke of the "Fasting Mind," the Mind that loses a little each day. Here we must remember that "Mind" is a translation of the Chinese word "Hsin" (Japanese "Kokoro"), which also means "Heart" and "Spirit." So he is speaking of the Fasting Heart-Mind-Spirit that gradually loses all excess and reduces itself to Essence. Growing up is, of course, the process of elimination, not adding to what we have. Each moment of the past must be burned to ashes for the present to exist unconditioned. This means moving from the habitual to the spontaneous and from the artificial to the natural. In effect, we retrace our steps.

Sunya, meaning Void or Great Emptiness, was an active concept in Indian philosophy long before Sakyamuni (the Buddha) was born. It was a Void of vastly different meaning from that of Zen, however, the Buddhist Sunyata. Traditional Indian Sunya was a place of spotless purity, a transcendental land far removed from the everyday world. While the Arhat of traditional Hinayana Buddhism wanted to escape from the burning forest of the world, the Zen person of Mahayana doesn't see it the same way. "Let me be reborn as a water buffalo and work for the farmer!" implores the dying Zen Master. And the Bodhisattva of Mahayana and Zen says, "If there are suffering creatures in Hell, let me go into Hell and save them!" Heaven and Hell are creations of Mind, too, and are relative in nature. At the bottom of all this is great Emptiness, for Heaven and Hell, too, do not have their own enduring self-nature.

"Vast Emptiness and Nothing Holy About It!" was Master Bodhidharma's reply to the Chinese emperor when the latter asked about the "Holy Truth." And within that Emptiness (Fullness?) we find mountains and rivers, suffering people and joyous people.

"Although I preached for forty-nine years, leading numerous beings to Salvation, in truth no one was led to Salvation and I never said a word," exclaimed the Buddha before he died, pointing to the fundamental emptiness of all phenomena.

"From the beginning not a thing is!" was Hui-neng's astounding statement. Of course, there is suffering! But one who suffers has no individual, lasting identity. In truth, who is the sufferer? At bottom, that one is empty too.

"Show me your mind and I will pacify it," promised Bodhidharma to his first disciple.

"But that's just it, I can't find it!" protested the disciple.

"There, I have pacified it for you!" triumphantly exclaimed the master.

When we look closely at dharmas (phenomena), we
always find they are dependent on something else, like the three
legs of a tripod. We have been brought up to believe in an
Eternal Soul. Buddhism says it is not so. Habit energies and
tendencies transmigrate from life to life, yet they are empty of
any nature of their own. Causes bring effects, and both cause
and effect, too, are empty. It was my surprising experience to
find that all things are as they have always been.

Thus, this Emptiness, this Void, becomes a great subject
of meditation in Zen. Zen teachers point out that the Void is not
relative Void; it is Absolute Emptiness, which some may cognize
as Absolute Being. "That home which is nowhere is the true
home!" There we find ourselves, and from Absolute Void come
Heaven, Earth and Humankind, as well as the 10,000 things of
the world.

It takes courage to face this meditation because we give
up everything of value we have ever clung to, including our own
supposed identity! In his "Sutra of Complete Enlightenment," the
Buddha warned that there will be few who are not terrified at this
great Truth. Rather would we keep the illusion of something on
which to lean; and yet, the Buddha said, "Be a lamp unto
yourself. Work out your own Salvation!"

The most difficult time comes when we have relin-
quished, one by one, all cherished things, leaving us only
Emptiness, for it will then be necessary to forsake this Emptiness
too. After all, Emptiness is also empty. In Kegon Buddhist
philosophy, the end of the long road of negation is the negation
of negation itself! In traditional Indian philosophy, one says,
"Neti, neti — not this, not that." All categories are disposed of
and when we can eliminate no more, that must be the Real. The
Sufi teachers said somewhat the same thing when they declared

that only what you have left after you have lost everything in a shipwreck actually belongs to you.

Zen Masters ask their disciples to act out of Emptiness, yet this Void is not suggested as a subject of meditation. Doing Shikan-taza (just Meditation), the very abstraction will eventually lead us to the experience of this Void, which is not over there apart from the things of the world over here, but is the Absolute Void containing all dharmas while, itself, being devoid of self-nature.

Taking Zen Meditation in the broader sense, I recommend this Sunyata as a subject for meditation and as something the aspirant is going to have to come to grips with sooner or later. Of course, there are those who feel Zen practice should just be Zazen, and who counsel us to deal only with abstraction, but this was not the Chinese way of the glorious days. If one will carefully read "The Scripture of the Sixth Patriarch" (the "Altar Sutra") one will find little about sitting in quietude. Hui-neng spoke of the spontaneous Prajna (Wisdom) of the straight-forward mind, as opposed to the traditional Dhyana practice of previous periods. He certainly dealt with the Great Vehicle, not the Small One.

Often we speak of "The Light Within." Some Taoists and some Buddhist mystics have spoken of this light as being like "black lacquer." The term "light" can be misleading, just as the term "emptiness" can be just a word with semantic meaning. Words are symbols, accepted by us to mean what they actually do not mean. To break through the relative concept of Void and actually experience this Emptiness, which will not be apart from things of the world, is the task of the Zen meditator. How to do this is something one will have to determine for oneself.

Chapter 7
NOT "EITHER-OR" BUT "NEITHER-NOR"

Zen is said to be:
> A special transmission without scripture,
> Beyond words and letters,
> Pointing directly to the Mind-Essence of man,
> Seeing into one's own Nature and knowing one's self as Buddha.

We read much about "Satori" in Zen books, but, strangely, the Japanese word "Kensho" is seldom mentioned. While a Zen answer might be that "Kensho is just Kensho," such a statement is not suitable for a book such as this, and the word "Kensho" is simply another symbol. Actually, attainment of Kensho represents the full Enlightenment of realizing one's own Buddha Nature, as opposed to the experience of the Great Joy, Satori, which may often be (as in the instance of Hakuin's first Satori) only a partial experience. Japanese Zen teachers say that Bodhidharma, the first Chinese patriarch, never used the name Zen (or Ch'an) at all, but referred to this strange religion as "Bushinshu," which might be roughly translated as "the Way of the Buddha" or "the Way of Buddha Nature." Suffice to say, the four-line description of Zen, above, is broad enough to include everything in Buddhism, while pointing to the experience itself instead of a study about the experience. Zen is ontological, not philosophic, in makeup, and demands that one have one's own realization, no matter how it jibes with what others have felt and said. This is why meditation, where we directly face the self-mind, is the most important key in Zen, as it generally should be in all Self-Power Buddhism.

A very helpful meditation subject in Buddhism, though not one that newcomers in Zen often encounter, is the so-called "Four-Cornered Negation" that is the cornerstone of the Middle Way. Since we are examining Zen Meditation in the broadest sense, and not just limiting our examination to Zazen, there is reason to believe that discussion of this key point of Buddhism, the Four-Cornered Negation, is in order. It must be well understood that the Buddha never taught in dualities, and one who sticks with ordinary dualistic thinking can never reach Zen Kensho in ten kalpas. Yet Zen is not monistic, either. When Hakuin, in his "Song of Dhyana" previously quoted, talks about a way of "non-duality" and "non-trinity," he is kicking over all the sacred shibboleths of orthodox religion and pointing at the fact that there are no categories under which to subsume the Zen experience. This must be well understood and meditated upon, and the following may help to make it clear:

When we ask questions about Zen, we are demanding a logical "either-or" answer. But Zen experience is not logical and the Zen world can be better understood as "neither-nor"*. This is why so much of what has been written about Zen by those inexperienced in its subtleties has no flavor of the Real about it. It is smooth, often glib, and entirely logical, and we easily understand the "either-or" explanations. But true Zen writing — usually limited to notes, made by disciples, of the Master's

---

*It was Genjun Sasaki, holding the chair of Indian Buddhism at Kyoto's Otani University, who first interested me in this neither-nor approach.

answers to questions — is from the heart of the alogical experience, and so often seems nonsense or gibberish to our logically-functioning minds. It is not for nothing that the Zen Masters have said, "The last thing a Zen monk should worry about is understanding." The taste of chocolate has nothing to do with an explanation of its history and properties.

To continue the "neither-nor" contrast, let's take a Buddhist answer to whether something is existent or not:

"It is neither existent nor non-existent, it is not a combination of existence and non-existence, and it is not a lack of existence and non-existence."

In this way we have eliminated all possible categories with one ruthless blow, and this puts an end to all discursive thinking; there is no direction for the mind to go. This is why the Zen Master has no worries about being consistent. One day he contradicts what he said the day before, and another day he claims both statements were wrong. He is constantly pulling the rug out from under the feet of the disciple, who is trying to anchor his or her "knowledge" in an "either-or" category. The Master won't give that person a chance, cutting off the budding concept in whatever way necessary, including the use of blows. Zen Masters are not sadistic, and yet we read of "cruel" shouting and beating. It is the quickest way to jolt the mind out of any of the categories of "is," "is not," "both is and is not," and "neither is nor is not." In Zen terminology, what is left after such a startling interruption is merely void — but this void is not emptiness (nor is it not emptiness). We are pulled, willy-nilly, into the world of "neither-nor."

So one day the Master declares, "The Mind is Buddha!" and the next day he tears this down with, "The Mind is not Buddha!" Woe to the disciple who repeats the Master's words back to him, dead in the disciple's mouth.

One time the Chinese Zen Master, Tokuzan, was walking through the hallway of his monastery, accompanied by a young attendant. The sound of bitter quarreling was heard, and soon the master came to the spot where two monks were having a strong disagreement. He waited patiently for an explanation.

The first monk said the Master had instructed so-and-so, and now this other fellow was trying to do just the opposite. He had explained the Master's words to the unruly culprit, but to no avail.

"Am I wrong?" asked the explaining monk.

Tokuzan shook his head. "You are right," he proclaimed.

The other monk was startled and immediately launched into a counter-offensive, explaining why he believed such-and-such to be the case.

"You also are right," the Master conceded, much to the amazement of his young attendant, who had just heard two contradictory points of view both labeled correct.

"But they surely can't both be right," blurted out the young attendant.

Tokuzan smiled. "And I perceive that you, too, are right," was his judgment.

Such contradiction cannot be categorized under "either-or." The monks would not dream of questioning the wisdom of the Master; yet, how could they accept the incident as totality unless they were willing to leave the world of logic and enter the "neither-nor" arena?

The great Chinese Zen Master, Chao Chou (Joshu in Japanese) was asked by a monk, "If a man comes, carrying nothing, what shall we tell him?"

"Tell him to throw it out!" was the immediate answer.

"But if he is carrying nothing, how can he throw it out?" protested the monk, quite logically.

"In that case, tell him to carry it out!" was the Master's sharp response.

Where is there any place for the logical intellect to grasp? After a while, the monk will give up the "either-or" aspect of questioning and sink his whole being into the experience itself, which has no categories but is just as it is.

The Zen student is not asked to think of this as part of the Middle Way (Madhyamika) of Buddhism, nor should one be confused by statements of "Mind Only" and "Mere Ideation" from other schools of Buddhism. For practical purposes of practice, Buddhism is Buddhism and Zen represents the purest kind of true Buddhist practice. Whether one is striving to be a Bodhisattva, in accordance with the urgings of Mahayana Buddhism, or is simply pursuing one's own Enlightenment, the Arhat Way of Hinayana Buddhism, the difference is really only skin deep.

"Are there truly other beings to save?" I asked a Zen Master one day.

The other, amused, answered evasively, "That's an interesting question, and we must talk about it sometime."

In truth, our Enlightenment *is* the saving of all beings. Ramana Maharshi, the great South Indian teacher, asked if, when you awaken from a dream, you inquire as to whether the others in the dream have also awakened! We need not split hairs over different classifications of Buddhism. One step begins the journey, and the Zen student should move right ahead, pausing for nothing, neither God nor Buddha. Such spirit will take care of all questions.

Until one understands the meaning of this Four-Cornered Negation, which the Buddha talked about so often in the Sutras, one will always be dealing in dualisms. Now, we cannot live in this world without being dualistic. Words are dualistic, including the Zen Master's words, and can be, at best, like a finger pointing at the moon. But is not the moon, though seen in different ways in all the lakes, ponds, rivers, and oceans of the world, still just the moon? We must not get hung up on dualisms and other classifications. There is a unity to all life, and there is a recognizable multiplicity to all life. In meditation we must bore ahead in such a way as to go beyond these, and this Meditation of the Four Negations can be a great help.

Chapter 8
THE LOTUS BLOSSOMS IN THE MUD
(fish do not live in clear water)

In India it is felt that contemplation of open space helps us to free the mind. It is easy to find wide vistas on the Indian sub-continent, but almost impossible in tiny Japan. Nevertheless, contemplation of a mountain stream, of the leaves changing color in autumn, and of the broad expanse of blue sky can help the introspective mind to free itself from its tendencies and dwell in the pure abstraction of Being (in Japan, moon-viewing is traditional, and there is certain special "moon-viewing food" to be eaten as one gazes from the "moon-viewing room").

We are told that the Zen Patriarch Engo declared:

> A shining sun in the clear blue sky, with no sense of East or West.
>
> Opposed, we have Time and Cause and Effect, and the medicine is prescribed according to the illness.
>
> Which is better — to release or to hang on — grasping or freeing?

The shining sun in the cloudless blue sky, with no feeling of direction (polarity), of course, represents the Absolute. There is no sense of here-and-there, of duality, or even of oneness. It just is, unhampered.

Contrasted to this is the world of cause-and-effect, where the teacher must use "expedient means" to fit the situation. There is no single Dharma to preach; depending on conditions, the teacher uses the necessary antidote, ruling out nothing.

Now, which is preferable, this spotless blue sky or the world of smog and smoke, dirt and passion, injustice and misery?

From the traditional East Indian viewpoint, we avoid the impure and look for the Absolute. We remove ourselves from the world of humankind and try to establish ourselves in some transcendental state.

But this is not the view of Zen at all. Samsara *is* Nirvana, there are no Buddhas apart from beings. The Life Force, our Divinity, is right here in the hearts of humans, greedy and angry though they may be. The lotus blooms in the slime and fish live only in contaminated, germ-filled water. Life does not exist in a vacuum. This is one of the greatest realizations that can come out of Zen training; it is all Here Now, and there is no place else to go. When the dying teacher of South India, Ramana Maharshi, was asked where he would go after death, he answered, "Where can I go? I'm here."

Zen meditation must not be dualistic and seek the pure state of the spotless blue sky. Nevertheless, contemplation of the limitless reaches of space can be a powerful abstract meditation. Zazen in empty places can be strong, but we must always come back to the world of beings.

In the ancient capitol of Kyoto, Japan, there are over 1600 Buddhist temples. Not all are Zen temples, but some of the most famous are. At Ryoanji is the rock garden that has been photographed so often; just a broad expanse of raked gravel, small pebbles, and a few "islands" of large stones. Many have interpreted this expanse from a worldly standpoint, calling these mountains and that an ocean and this a land mass. But the monk contemplating this garden does not see it in such a mundane way. It is not nature — actually, being so completely planned, it is the very opposite of natural — and it is not artificial. The arrangement looks inevitable. It speaks of something beyond design — not asymmetrical but "beyond symmetry." We can lose ourselves in it without definition. The Sanskrit word "Tathata" (Suchness) comes to mind. Meditating at such a place, we see and we do not see. There is an echo, but of what voice we do not know. "I know that I do not know," says the Sage, and this is the real knowing. Having no definition, we suffer no boundaries.

Many other temples in Kyoto are fit places for outside abstract meditation. Almost my favorite is Saiho-ji (called "Kokadera" by many because of the numerous different kinds of moss that cover the area). It is hard to believe that someone willfully planted the rocks, caused the stream to flow, and stationed the trees so that the varied colors of autumn would blaze as they do, but it was all meticulously planned. We have the feeling of enormous space, when, in truth, the area covered is not very large. Nobody waters the moss underfoot. According to the season we have rain or we don't, and the natural aspects change with each rainfall. Little sun penetrates the dense foliage, and it is very cold in winter to wander through Saiho-ji (preferably at a time when not too many parties of school children are present) and to allow ourselves time to contemplate is to return to something primeval. One photographer captioned his pictures of Saiho-ji with: "Speaking more of Eternity than of the ephemeral world of man."

But that's just the point — the ephemeral world of humans *is* Eternity. Patriarch Engo's cloudless blue sky is not apart from the world of cause-and-effect. When we sit in meditation at Saiho-ji we must not see it as beauty and purity apart from life. It is as it is.

There is great variety in the temples of Kyoto. To the Western Zen student visiting that city, it is recommended that one sit in Zazen in as many as possible. Take a streetcar to the countryside and you will find a few almost-deserted temples overrun with untended natural growth. For the unhurried, there is time for contemplation of the change incessantly taking place (Anicca — "impermanence" in Sanskrit), and a feeling of something behind the change. It is easy to understand how the great Haiku poet, Basho, found inspiration in that countryside. To be there is enough, if we are really there.

In Kyoto and nearby Nara we will find scrolls of the Chinese monk Mu-chi ("Mokke" in Japanese), hanging in some places and stored in others. No one has better expressed the Zen way in picture. The "Rembrandt of the Orient," Sesshu, was a monk at Shokoku-ji in Kyoto, and his work, so skillfully wrought in several radically different styles ("Suiboku," etc.), takes us through the seasons as one Life Force pervades them all. If we see the wonderful picture of a large bird (a cormorant?) done in ink by Miyamoto Musashi (not a painter but Japan's greatest swordsman, a Samurai much influenced by Zen), we have a feeling of the "Potentiality" Zen teachers speak of. On "Mushi Boshi," the one day of the year when temples air out their hidden treasures (if the weather is not damp), we can find unknown wonders that speak of something far beyond the form sketched out by the artist. Viewing form, we transcend form. Seeing the garden, we perceive something formless behind the forms.

"When we realize that Form is the Form of the Formless, our singing and dancing takes place nowhere but where we are," says Hakuin Zenji. We must not try to separate this "Formless" from the Form, however. In Zen, it is right in the Form that we observe the Formless, and the Formless returns us to Form.

"If all things return to the One, to what does the One return?" asks the Koan.

Why, to the Many, of course. Each speaks of the other. "If we were not chilled in winter, could the plum blossoms of spring be so fragrant?" asks the Master. Can we have Up without Down? Hui-Neng, the Sixth Patriarch, tells us that such opposites indicate the Mean. So the cloudless blue sky and the smoggy, human-polluted air of the cities — they are not two different things. When we perceive this, we can follow our own way without hindrance. No two snow crystals are alike; no two beings are the same. Yet they are not unalike.

There is a well-to-do university teacher in Kyoto who maintains a private gallery upstairs in his spacious house. One can go there only by invitation. Tea is served in a formal Cha-No-Yu (Tea Ceremony), and the visitor's behavior is carefully observed. No one pays attention to the extreme cold; there is no central heating and no strong sunlight to warm things. Once a month — or every other month — the host changes his "exhibition," hanging new scrolls and displaying new artifacts.

And what treasures! Here is a scroll by Musashi's teacher, the man who imparted Zen to Japan's legendary Samurai. There are two drawings by Zen Master Sengai, and one by Hakuin himself. Here is calligraphy by the penniless monk, Ryokan, perhaps Japan's best-known calligrapher. There is nothing trivial in the collection.

And all this speaks of — what? What do these works have in common? What makes them suitable for hanging by this connoisseur?

It is true that, here, we see an effete Japan at work. There is a "dandyism" that counters the trend to modernization in Japan. The friend, a shop owner, who took me to the "museum" home the first time, wore a kimono, as did the host — not just any kimonos but almost ceremonial robes. The articles used in the Tea Ceremony were properly "Shibui" (I cannot define this austere, understated feeling), and the conduct of visitor and host was almost priestlike. Yet, in a larger sense, it was reassuring. Ancient values have not disappeared; the work of the Men-of-Truth who did the creating lives on. In a short time after leaving the gallery-home, the two visitors found themselves back on a noisy streetcar on their way to a prosaic lunch, but for a moment, there was a timeless world that only three were able to view. The host was delighted that the foreigner was properly awed by his collection. Who had expected to look inside Sengai and Hakuin on such a cold grey winter's morning?

Such works of art, touched with Zen, can lead us to real contemplation. In medieval Japan, fortunes were often spent to give a teahouse a properly impoverished and rustic look! This speaks of a people who worship understatement, and there is so much of Zen in such an attitude.

Though I have listed the attributes of a Zen garden in another book* I am going to repeat them here. This is not my translation, nor my own compilation, and I cannot even give credit for it as I do not know who did the work. But the seven points should be valid for Zen study. They speak of "Wabi Sabi," which is Japanese with Zen overtones. How to define "Wabi Sabi"? No one knows. But my students all agree that the gate at Miajima is *not* "Wabi Sabi" — it is too new and bright. The same is true of Kyoto's Golden Pavilion (Kinkakuji). After a hundred years of being stained by time, perhaps both will acquire this desired characteristic, but they are too new and flashy for the Japanese Zen taste at this time. One should keep this in mind when digesting the following characteristics of the Japanese Zen garden:

---

*Climb the Joyous Mountain/Living the Meditative Way

FUKINSEI — asymmetry or dissymetry; suggesting things which are irregular. The opposite of geometric circles or squares.

KANSO — simplicity; without gaudiness, not heavy or gross; clean, neat, and fresh, yet reserved, frank, and truthful; not ornate.

KOKO — austerity, maturity, reduction to essentials; lack of sensuousness; refers to things that are aged, weathered, venerable; like "Wabi Sabi."

SHIZEN — naturalness, artlessness, absence of pretense and artificiality. It does not mean raw nature; it involves full creative intent, but should not be forced; unselfconsciousness; true naturalness that is a negation of the naive and accidental.

YUGEN — subtly profound; suggestion rather than total revelation; things not wholly revealed but partly hidden from view; shadow and darkness; hence, Yugen involves the shadow areas of the garden.

DATSUZEKU — unworldliness; freedom from use of "compasses and rulers;" freedom from worldly attachments, bondage, and restrictive laws. It involves transcendence of conventional usage. It is often a surprise element or an astonishing characteristic.

SEIJAKU — quietness, calmness, and silence; opposite of disturbance. In the Orient there is a saying that "Stillness is Activity." This characteristic should be strongly felt in a Japanese garden.

Conclusion: In summary, the basic philosophy of the Japanese garden is about the same as the seven principles of Zen. A free translation of them appears above. It is interesting to add that flowers are seldom used as decoration, it being strongly felt that they have a special life of their own. Such respect for all things, animate and inanimate, is characteristic of Zen.

In Zen there has never been a valid difference between a monk and a lay person. There is no "hidden" teaching — Zen is Zen, not knowledge to be acquired but "the straightforward mind as it is." Whichever way of life we follow, the result is the same. Actually, the East Indian layman Vimalakirti (the name means "Spotless Purity") was one of the most respected of Buddhist teachers, and the "Sutra Spoken by Vimalakirti" is one of the favorites of Zen Masters. In China, of course, many Sages were government administrators; there was no line of demarcation between the Worldly and the Cloistered. To know is to know, and it has nothing to do with the mode of existence.

One time a Zen Master was quietly meditating when a traveling monk unexpectedly appeared. Immediately the Master drew a circle in the dirt and then placed the Chinese character for Water in the center.   Looking at the monk quizzically, the master noted that the traveler did not at all understand.

Very often in Zen temples, we find a hanging scroll (kakemono) with just a circle and some writing on the side. The character for Water — perhaps signifying Purity — was so much icing on the cake. The circle was enough.

Once a Master asked his monks an elaborate question about someone up a tree, hanging by his teeth from a branch while wild animals waited below to eat him if he fell. At this moment, the one hanging from the tree is asked a Zen question. If he does not answer, he fails. But how can he open his mouth?

None of the monks could solve this impossible situation, but a thoroughly enlightened visitor stepped forward and boldly stated, "Never mind the man hanging from the branch. Tell me something about him *before* he climbed the tree!" The Master chuckled.

This pointing at essentials, refusing to be sidetracked by "meaningless" phenomena, is characteristic of the open space and the art mentioned in this chapter. A lonely bird on a dead branch in winter: what has this to say to us? Obviously something. What that something is I will leave the reader to find out in his or her meditation. It is not a thing; yet it is Something.

Stepping out the temple gate in the brilliant moonlight, we find ourselves on an uneven path of stones leading across the temple grounds. The tall trees screen the slanting temple roof, which does not glare in the bright moonlight. It is cold! But we have already established that fact and there is no need to think of it again. Losing ourselves in the setting, there is no discomfort. If we are too full of self, we suffer with the cold.

Overhead the stars, and underneath, we sense the moist earth. And yet, in the distance we hear a streetcar rattling along the tracks, and, close by, automobiles and motorcycles roar past the temple on Karasuma Street, one of Kyoto's principal thoroughfares. The purity of our solitary temple-sitting blends with the busy city sounds beyond, and there is a real meaning. What is that meaning? Who is there to know it?

Chapter 9
THE BUDDHA OF INFINITE LIGHT
(how pure is the Pure Land?)

In Japan, the Obaku Zen sect uses the Nembutsu usually associated with Shin Buddhism. Chinese Zen Masters of the past, and even a few in Japan, have not hesitated to use this device of "Other Power" Buddhism when the temperament of the Zen aspirant seemed to call for it. Perhaps it would be useful to take a look at the "Pure Land" sect ("Shin," or "Jodo Shinshu" in Japan) in order to better understand the discipline that is used and to decide whether it could be part of our meditation practice.

The "Amitabha" cult of Buddhism began in India, but it really came to fruition after traveling to China. At one time the "Pure Land" school, supposedly founded by the Chinese Hui-Yuan, had a powerful hold on the religious imagination of China. "Kuan-Yin" ("Kwannon" in Japan, the Buddhist "Bodhisattva of Mercy") is a female in China and Japan, but was the male Bodhisattva, Avalokitesvara, in India. Because of the sentiment attached to a "Goddess of Mercy," Kuan-Yin had a powerful hold on many Chinese, as Kwannon does today in Japan, and eventually became firmly associated with the "Other Power Pure Land" school. It is doubtful if any other Buddhist figure emotionally stirs Chinese and Japanese imagination as much as this great symbol of mercy who does not judge but only saves. Since this, too, is the activity of the "Amitabha" sect ("Amida" in Japan), it is easy to see how Chinese and Japanese associated the Buddha of Infinite Light (Amitabha, Amida) and the "Goddess of Mercy." Sinner and saint are to be saved; all who suffer must receive succor, without distinction.

Aeons ago a great Bodhisattva in India took massive vows, including the one to save all sentient beings. This Bodhisattva then became the Buddha of Infinite Light (not historic). Sakyamuni, who lived 2500 years ago in his "Form Body," was, as Buddha, a manifestation of this Buddha of Infinite Light.

These great vows, taken unthinkable millions of year ago, are still in effect. Since we mortals in this "Dharma-Declining" age are too weak to lead ascetic lives, meditate, and work out our own salvation (as counseled by Gautama Buddha), Amitabha has arranged to take us to "The Pure Land" or "Western Paradise" when we die, and there we will find conditions ideal for reaching Enlightenment. All we have to do is remember and believe in the saving grace of the Buddha of Infinite Light. We do this, in Japan, by repeating the Nembutsu, NAMU AMIDA BUTSU (Hail to the Buddha of Infinite Light) not once, not a thousand times, but constantly until it has impressed itself on our consciousness and the Nembutsu goes on automatically in our purified hearts.

This, of course, is "Other Power Buddhism." We are relying on the power of another, just as the Christian may do with Jesus, instead of relying on ourselves and working out our own salvation as Sakyamuni advised. In many ways such surrender has more in common with Christianity than with traditional Buddhism, but there are great differences. By remembering, the good are saved and the bad are saved. There is no wrathful God waiting to pass judgment. I am weak and cannot meditate to reach salvation as the strong Zennists do. I have sinned and can only believe Amida's great saving vow will wipe out my sins and take me to the Western Paradise — if I can only get my little self out of the way.

And here is where the two branches come together. In his or her great ascetic practice, the Zen man or woman eliminates the small ego center that has separated him or her from everything else; the Jodo Shinshu devotee does the same thing with surrender. In some ways this is comparable to Indian Bhakti (Devotion) as opposed to Raja Yoga (the eight steps leading to suppression of mind and tendencies in Samadhi).

So, at the deepest level there is much in Shin Buddhism to interest the Zen person. Often masters have stated that, when deviousness has been eliminated from the mind and one no longer is ruled by greed, anger, and delusion, the simple, straightforward mind *is* the Pure Land. Resting in our own nature, we have reached the Western Paradise.

Some intellectual Shin Buddhists understand the teaching in this manner, that we are dealing with levels of consciousness and the term "Pure Land" is allegorical. However, the vast majority believe in the teaching on a very literal basis and hope to be taken to the great Western Paradise by the power of Amida's primeval vow. They are rather fuzzy about the efforts that will be required of them after reaching the Pure Land, often thinking of it as a more-or-less permanent Paradise in the Christian sense.

The Japanese writer, D.T. Suzuki, was supposed to have been a Shin Buddhist all his life, though he popularized Zen in the West. He is said to have declared that more cases of Satori develop in Japan from the simple repetition of the Nembutsu than from all the strenuous exertions of Zen practice. This is quite possible as about one-half of all Japanese Buddhists (if we don't count the militaristic and quasi-political Soka Gakkai as "Buddhist") belong to one form or another of Shin Buddhism.

Shin Buddhism, in Japan, was founded in the twelfth century by the fascinating Honen, who supposedly became a

monk when his aristocratic father, having been struck down by
another, pleaded with his son on his death bed *not* to think of
revenge but to enter the Buddhist priesthood to work for the
salvation of his assassin! It is a wonderful story, though how
true we cannot be sure.

One of the most appealing figures in all Eastern religious
history was Shinran (1173-1262), a Christ-like Japanese who
spent many vain years meditating in the great Buddhist monastery on the top of Mount Hiei outside Kyoto. The harder he tried
with "Self Power," the more he failed. Then, descending the
mountain, this great figure — who was not a monk and not a lay
person — became the disciple of Honen, put aside the power of
his own little ego self, and, trusting in the Saving Power of
Amida, spent the rest of his life (partly in exile) spreading the
teaching of Jodo Shinshu to the simple country people of Japan.
His great travail, a true Dark Night of the Soul, was beautifully
described by Shinran's grandson as follows:

> Many moons passed as he practiced contempla-
> tion on the moon of the three-fold Truth in the ten-stage
> meditation, and the seasons' flowers renewed their
> fragrance many times as he disciplined himself in
> pondering on the Truth of one hundred worlds with one
> thousand modes of Suchness. Then he reflected on the
> problem of Salvation and thought: "However hard I may
> try to calm the water of meditation, waves of conscious-
> ness arise to disturb it. However hard I may try to
> contemplate the moon of mind-nature, clouds of illusion
> overcast it."

Once Shinran came to the Saving Grace of Amida, he
repeated the simple "Namu Amida Butsu, Namu Amida Butsu"

for the rest of the days of his life, all doubt completely extinguished by his faith in the Saving Grace of the Buddha of Infinite Light.

Shinran's great heart can be perceived in his words: "Unhindered in space like the light cloud, free from all impediments, none is there unblessed by the light. Take refuge in the Inconceivable One."

If we remember Zen Master Dogen's admonition: "To train and enlighten all things from self is delusion; to train and enlighten the self from all things is Enlightenment," I believe it will be easy to see how, for the proper devotional temperament, the Nembutsu practice can be favorable. It is a prime way to remove the troublesome self, so that only Buddha, and no self, remains in the heart.

It is very touching in Japan to come upon whole families devotedly chanting together: "Namu Amida Butsu, Namu Amida Butsu." It can be a lazy man's way, as Shin Buddhists give up nothing of the secular life, or, for the sincere, it can be a raft to the other shore.

I have included "Namu Amida Butsu" in this book of Zen Meditation because there may be practitioners who are attracted to the Way of Devotion. For the right person, such selfless chanting can be powerful, and it must be remembered that Obaku Zen uses the Nembutsu. Over the centuries many Zen Masters have made use of it.

One Ch'an (Chinese Zen) Master of Modern Times asked his students, when sitting Zazen, to mentally repeat the word "Amitabha." Then they were to be silent for a bit, following which they repeated the name of the Buddha of Infinite Light.

Something, or somebody, was repeating the name, he pointed out. Who was that one? This reminds us of the teaching of Zen Master Basui, who wanted to know, "Who was the Boss?" Who was this "Man of No Title" (as Rinzai referred to him) who actually repeated Amitabha's name? Who heard the silent sound? Where did the sound originate, and where did it finally dissolve?

This is somewhat like the T'ien T'ai "Chih-Kuan" meditation, and it is very powerful. Such mental uttering of the Name, followed by mental silence, will drive away all other thoughts. And then, when we utter the name again (it doesn't matter whether it is Amitabha or the Japanese Amida), it rings out in the emptiness like a temple bell.

"Amitabha, Am-i-taaaa-bha." Where does it come from: There is origination, there is dissolution. Can we find the source? This is literally looking for the "Essence of this mind," as Basui instructed.

If we choose, we can say the whole Nembutsu (Namu Amida Butsu) mentally and then carry on the meditation. I believe that using the Nembutsu, or just the Buddha's name, in this manner, is in strict accord with the principles of Zen practice.

The words of the "Lotus Sutra" — NAMU MYO HO RENGE KYO — were first popularized in Japan by the militant thirteenth century monk, Nichiren, and they are chanted by all branches of Nichiren Buddhism (including Soka Gakkai), as well as by some of the independent so-called "New Religions" of Japan. The Nichiren sect is now becoming very popular in America, and, undoubtedly, the Zen aspirant will be exposed to this chanting (the "Lotus Sutra" has always been a Zen favorite too), though Nichiren himself was a great enemy of Zen in Japan.

Chapter 10
CONCLUSION
(which is just a beginning)

Zen Meditation is not therapy. It is not the purpose of Zazen to effect an adjustment to society, nor does Zen Meditation aim at making one "feel good." Indeed, unless one is stirred deeply in the subconscious — particularly if working with a Koan in Rinzai Zen — there is little chance of lasting progress.

Though one may experience improved health or find that one is thinking more clearly and able to face problems more easily, these are merely fringe benefits that accrue from the practice of Zen Meditation. They do not represent the true results. One must reach the Satori experience and know the taste of Enlightenment. So many Masters have pointed out that, though meditation practice is cumulative, the Great Joy Experience of Satori is unpremeditated and instantaneous. One does not "feel it coming on," and it cannot be deliberately cultivated. Those who have experienced Satori often state that the Great Joy is more like a remembering of what has been forgotten than the act of learning something new. And then, after the Great Experience, with its joy and tears, one must continue cultivation to the point of Kensho, complete identification with the Buddha Nature.

To practice Zen Meditation does not demand any faith other than the confidence that one *does* have one's own True

Nature, and that this will be uncovered in its own good time. A doubting, iconoclastic attitude, except in the practice of Nembut-su, can be helpful. One will note changes taking place, both physical and mental, and others will also notice them, but these are concomitants, fingers pointing at the moon and not the moon itself. To go off on side trips, no matter how intriguing, is to be avoided. It is best to forget what one has read concerning miracles and so-called powers. In fact, if one could forget all reading and simply be aware of the Buddha's basic pronounce-ments, practice would be easier. A few key realizations of Gautama Buddha are helpful, such as:

All is temporary and changing every second, which can readily be ascertained by close observation. This impermanence, Anicca, is quite opposed to the state of mind of the average person, who acts as though he or she is immortal and whatever good fortune one possesses will always endure.

Though there is pain and pleasure, there is no lasting entity experiencing these. It is hard to get away from "I" and "Mine" and realize that there are impersonal processes going on. Though I have been brought up to believe that I have an eternal soul, arbitrarily created by a personal God, the Truth of Bud-dhism is that there is no lasting "I" and no real "other." The five "heaps" — "skandhas" in Sanskrit — give the appearance of an ego center where, in truth, there is none. These five conditions are: Form, Feelings, Perceptions, Emotional Impulses and Consciousness. All arise when conditions are right and subside when proper conditions are absent.

When the skandhas are erased, nothing remains of the "personality," the ego identity that seemed so permanent. There are habit-energies and tendencies ("vasanas" and "samskaras" in Sanskrit), and these go on from life to life, each cause resulting in an effect, but there is no central person experiencing them. The skandhas are not ours; we are a product of the skandhas.

This "An-Atman" teaching is, on the surface, contradictory to everything that had been taught in India before the Buddha.

Suffering — Dukkha — is universal. All beings suffer. Failure to accept the truth of impermanence and refusal to believe there is no eternal "I" will inevitably result in suffering. If we believe the beautiful mate we married will always be beautiful, and if we think the universe revolves around ourselves (in the smallest sense), we are bound to suffer.

Actually, the Buddha pointed out that Suffering is the result of Greed, Anger and Delusion. Greed means "lust" and it also means "gluttony." Anger takes in "annoyance" and it also includes "resentment," resentment at the very Karmic conditions we ourselves have created. Delusion means mistaking the unreal for the Real, believing that the temporary is permanent and lasting.

Thus, Suffering is universal. This is not the suffering of "pain" as opposed to "pleasure." "Pain" is suffering and, though it is hard to believe, "pleasure," too, will result in suffering. In orthodox Buddhism: "All this is ill," meaning that any individual and conditioned existence is suffering. However, Zen was much influenced by Chinese Taoism and parts dramatically from Indian Buddhism at this point. The Zen Master says, "Every day is a good day!" Life is not something from which to escape, as in traditional Buddhism, but something to be lived to the full with Compassion and with Joy. No one denies that beings suffer, but Zen does not feel such suffering is inevitable. Nevertheless, Zen is a Religion of Salvation, not a psychotherapy of social adjustment. The practitioner should keep his or her eye on the main chance. One's objective is nothing less than Total Enlightenment. Let the corollary benefits come, if they will. Let the psychic experiences multiply, if they do — we will ignore them. After all, they are products of one's own mind and just represent ignorance.

Many who have read books about Indian Yoga have come to believe that sensational psychic experiences represent spirituality. There are "teachers" who describe their visions to their disciples, much to the delight of the latter, who believe that sight of "other-worldly" creatures represents great wisdom.

This is not the way of Zen. The concentrated mind tends to dream less and have fewer visions. The beginner may be more troubled with Makyo than the experienced meditator. Total concentration may result in perception of a "blue star," or a swelling blue mass, the effect of the accumulation of Prana, but nothing more. If, in practice, the meditator sees the Buddha of Infinite Light floating toward him or her, with the Buddha's two attendant Bodhisattvas on either side, one ignores the sight. It is the sitter's own mind he or she is working with. Outside phenomena are just that, the product of one's own mind. Excessive visions and continued dreaming show a disturbed mind, and one who follows down this path in the mistaken view that it represents "Reality" will never attain a one-pointed mind. Total abstraction, with full awareness, is most indicative of the concentrated state, not the razzle-dazzle of glorious visions and thousand-sun splendor.

Buddhism is, in some ways, highly scientific. It asks you to evaluate the datum of your own experience without prejudice and without preconception. The Buddha was the first great psychologist, and the enlightened teachers who followed him went into profound analyses of the factors of consciousness in such advanced works as the Abidharma. While Zen practice does not go deeply into the philosophic and psychological aspects of meditation, preferring to let the experience be as it is, Zen teachers are well aware of the basic tenets of Buddhism and will inculcate their students with them whenever possible. Fundamentally, the Zen teachers will continue to pull the rug out from under the feet of the practitioner until the latter has lost all preconceptions and has nothing whatever to grasp. Only then will the student *know* the truth of "the home that is nowhere, that is the true home" and realize how Hui-neng was enlightened by the phrase "the non-abiding mind."

Each person's path is individual in Zen. No two snow crystals are alike, and no two people have the same temperament. Zen teachers well understand this.

There is a tendency, entirely justified, to decry the institutionalization of Zen and other religions. Zen writer Paul Reps calls today's organized Zen, in Japan, FRO-ZEN (frozen), a phrase he took from a Sufi teacher in San Francisco. Where there is too much regimentation, there is rigidity, and this totally annuls the true spontaneity that is Zen. Hitler's troops, goose-stepping in precision, were not practicing Zen. For this reason, some will want to go their own way, to practice Zen Meditation and reach the desired goals of Zen without having to bother with the ritual and conformity of institutionalized Zen. It is for these hardy souls that this book has been written. I bring my two palms together in a Gassho of respect and wish them well. Each person's Enlightenment *is* the saving of all beings.

Epilogue

As mentioned in a previous chapter, some years ago I spent a very enjoyable evening in Kyoto, Japan at the house of a famous scholar and university teacher, who is also considered a Roshi. Two scholars accompanied me, one Japanese and one American, who helped me considerably with translation when my own Japanese proved insufficient for the type of discussion being held. The Roshi is married and leads a "normal" householder's life — yet he is greatly respected in Japanese Buddhist circles (where monks often get married, in direct disregard of the monastic rules laid down by Pai Chang in China).

Continually, the master spoke of "The Formless Self." Indeed, his last admonition to me (a musician and composer) was to "write the music of the Formless Self." The teacher indicated that only in the music of the Noh theatre of Japan was such subliminal music heard, that which went beyond the mind directly to the subconscious.

After hearing about "The Formless Self" all evening, I began to wonder about the teachings of the Buddha, but at that time, I was too timid or too polite to question the Master. Repeatedly, the Buddha made it clear that there is no Self, that there is nothing abiding (as a Self would have to be), and that permanence, or permanent identity, did not exist and was not to be relied upon.

Yet here, suddenly, the Master had created a "permanent" Formless Self, perhaps meaning by it to refer to something like Lin-chi's (Rinzai's) "Man of No Title." This, in itself, is, of course, a duality — a "Formless Self" would be a dualism in contradistinction to "A Self with Form." No amount of dialectics will successfully explain that away.

Moreover, the Buddha had made it quite clear that there was no Self with Form, without Form, both with and without Form, or lacking both Form and absence of Form! This is the four-cornered negation, the foundation of the "Middle Way" of Buddhism, the very essence of the Mahayana teaching. And yet now, in Japan, Mahayana Buddhists were inventing a Formless Self to contradict everything the Buddha had taught. In traveling from India to China, and then to Korea and Japan, it is natural that much of the Buddha's original teachings have been discarded and local authorities have taken paths directly opposed to the original meaning of Indian Buddhism and the authority of the Sutras themselves. It seems natural for religions to eventually latch on to a "Self," no matter how they define it, and to think of it as the one unchanging Reality in all the Universe of Change.

The trouble is, we then begin to get into a Transcendentalism that is contrary to the Buddhist teaching. It is all here now, according to the Buddha, and we must have a body in order to work out Karma and to experience the Reality. No disembodied spirit, no transcendental "creature," and certainly no god (Deva), or other divine form, can come to complete Enlightenment; a body is needed for that. So Transcendentalism, the yearning for the "other-worldly," is hardly compatible with the teachings of Buddhism.

When we begin to get into such matters as "The Formless Self," we then follow through with the wonder of how this Essence, this Substance, takes on the world of Form. This Formless Self manifests as the rivers, the mountains, and the phenomena of the world, and we have the great mystery of how it can be Formless and yet show up as the 10,000 Things. And right here we begin to duplicate the Indian teachings of Brahmanism, or the Tantric Siva-Sakti.

In Tantra, Siva represents the undifferentiated Reality, but it is the Female Aspect, the Sakti, which manifests as World, as Power and as Consciousness. In conventional Hinduism, it is the formless Brahman that functions as the innumerable aspects of the world of Form, and is not in any way diminished by so doing. These are, of course, similar to the idea of a Formless Self (as expounded by the Zen Master) that is, itself, the Substance, and that functions as the world of humankind, of gods, and of all phenomena. We have thus brought Zen to a point where it is indistinguishable from other Indian teachings, though we may use slightly different terms. And there is nothing wrong with this; these are sublime beliefs that carry a good deal of weight and represent, to their followers, a degree of Truth.

But it was not the intent of Sakyamuni, the historic Buddha, to duplicate the teachings of his time and reinforce the beliefs then current. He made a radical departure from Indian tradition, saying there was no Atman, no permanent Soul, and no abiding Substance. Moreover, the Sixth Patriarch, Hui-neng, reached his Enlightenment while hearing a phrase from the "Diamond Sutra" that assures us of the "Non-Abiding Mind." That which abides nowhere is not a permanent "Self," Formless or otherwise. Indeed, the Buddha pointed to certain places known as the "Formless Heavens," where all present were disembodied; this hardly made them Enlightened or permanent, and their presence in Heaven was, according to Buddhist standards, a great handicap, as the continued experience of pleasure would take away any leaning toward final Emancipation. Somehow, only Suffering leads us to the wish for real Salvation.

So I must respectfully disagree with the Master's pronouncement, and with much of the Japanese Mahayana teachings that seem counter to the Buddha's exhortations. In

Zen, of course, we are more interested in the experience of Reality than all the theories about it. As soon as we use words, whether they are words such as "The Formless Self," or Gautama Buddha's own teachings, as recorded in the Sutras, we are telling lies or, at best, half-truths. These are meant as signposts pointing at the Real Experience, and they are a way of encouraging other Buddhists to plunge in and experience the Real themselves. As such, writings and teachings can be helpful; they bring many to the practice. Then they must be discarded, as must all concepts. The Formless Self is a concept and, as such, is a definite duality existing only in words.

This matter of An-Atman, the knowledge that there is no everlasting Self of any kind, is the stickiest and most difficult point in Buddhism. We are sure there is an entity that performs and one that is affected, and even present-day Zen teachers drift into the human delusion mentioned above — and it is the delusion of a persevering entity, the failure to accept that it is only the five "Heaps" (Skandhas) that give the appearance of a person, that makes suffering inevitable.

In this regard, it is said in Buddhism:

"Clear Comprehension of Reality is the clarity and knowledge that behind all functions there is no abiding personality, soul, ego, or substance."

In other words:

"Within there is no self that acts, and outside there is no self affected by the action."

The Zen student would do well to ponder this matter. Without acknowledging the truth of No-Ego — and then experiencing it in the Emptiness — the Zen aspirant cannot hope to realize a Buddhist Enlightenment.

The great Chinese Ch'an Master, Yun-Men, upon hearing a distant temple bell, exclaimed, "The Universe is so vast! Why does the sound of a bell range over only seven notes?"

He was referring to the seven emotions, declaring that living beings are at the mercy of Pleasure, Anger, Sorrow, Joy, Love, Hate, and Desire — it is these that limit us and bring about life after life of conditioned existence, which is Suffering.

When a Rinzai Zen monk is about to enter the Master's quarters for Sanzen, the "kill-or-be-killed" confrontation, he strikes a large bell twice to announce his entrance. There are an infinite number of ways in which to strike a bell two times. One can pause, make one sound louder than the other, rush the two together, or send these two sounds out into the wide universe in whatever way suits one's psyche at that exact moment. It is said that a true Master can tell the monk's state of mind simply by hearing these two sounds of the bell. As with Yun-men, he can detect the emotions beneath the monk's exterior and so deal with the aspirant in the way best for that person. Zen practice is highly individual, and the Master will eventually know more about the disciple than the latter can ever hope to know. As my former teacher remarked about a favored student who had been with him for three years, before the student suddenly left, "A little while longer and I believe he would have revealed to me what he *really* wants!"

Though the Chinese Hua-yen philosophy is not connected with Ch'an, this deep and abstruse teaching has much to offer the Zen meditator. In a revealing statement about the Absolute and the Relative (often referred to as "Host" and "Guest" by Ch'an adepts), Hua-yen says:

> When One is absorbed by All,
> One penetrates into All.
> When All is absorbed by One,
> One penetrates into One.

When One is absorbed by One,
One penetrates into One.
When All is absorbed by All,
All penetrates into All.

Finally, a few words in general about meditation. In India it is said that "a lamp does not flicker in a windless place." This is a description of Ekagra, the one-pointed state of mind. It is the Samadhi of the Buddhists. Is it a dull, apathetic state? Hardly. It is just the opposite. When the Buddha was asked if he was a god, he answered "no." Asked again what he was, he replied, "I am awake!" Few there are who are awake.

If we ask how meditation works, we are getting far from Zen because Zen is interested in the fact of meditation, not theories about it. Yet it may be helpful to the experienced meditator to hear what Indian Tantra (which has more in common with Zen than might be supposed) says about meditation:

When consciousness apprehends an object as different from itself, it sees that object as extended in space. But when the object is completely *subjectified*, it is experienced as an unextended point. This is true one-pointedness, the goal of all meditation.

Retrospective
(a personal commentary)

Sometimes it seems to me that Mahayana Buddhism is a separate religion, with little relationship to so-called "Primitive Buddhism" and the original teachings of Gautama Buddha. We must never forget that Zen *is* a Buddhist sect and that great Zen teachers have always spoken of the Line of Transmission from the Buddha on down to the present time. However, I am convinced that the Zen of India is apocryphal; that, while the Indian patriarchs *did* live, they did not think of themselves as "Zen Teachers" and that their so-called "Last Gathas" (the stanzas they spontaneously uttered before death) were compositions of a much later period, placed in their mouths in much the same way that Chinese scholars sanctify their own opinions by crediting them to the legendary sage-emperors of the past.

Certainly Zen, with its affirmation of life "just as it is," much more closely resembles the Taoism of China with which it was cross-fertilized. And Mahayana Buddhism's Tantric sect, with its conviction that each person is a potential reservoir of Joy, hardly echoes the pessimism of early Buddhist teaching. Theravada Buddhism agrees with the Buddha's exhortations that one cannot find satisfaction in this life or, indeed, in any individual existence; this is far from the Zen belief (echoed by Taoism) that, right here and now, life has meaning and can be rewarding if we go with the life current and do not oppose it. To find the Essence, as many Zen teachers have implored, and then to flow with that Essence, is to be the Buddha. Even the "instantaneous" enlightenment (the result of long periods of training) of Zen is far different from what the early Buddhist Sangha looked forward to. The world is an evil place, they believed, a mistake, and we should get out of it permanently — if necessary, sacrificing this whole life to the attainment of Nirvana. And this "Nirvana" (which has nothing to do with death, as many mistakenly think) is different in Original Buddhism, far from the "Samsara is Nirvana" concept of Zen and later Mahayana training.

I have heard a Zen Master repeatedly say, "God or Buddha or whatever name you give to Ultimate Authority." This was hardly the teaching of Original Buddhism. The Christian God, of course, is a Creator God, omnipotent and omnipresent; Sakyamuni Buddha never claimed to be the Creator, nor even a minor god. Asked what he was, he simply replied, "Awake!"

One of the greatest and most influential of Chinese Masters claimed that the Buddha was "The Essence of Being." There was a Mahayana belief (very limited in scope) that this world was simply the meditation of the Adya Buddha. Such abstractions not only do not fit in with the original concept of who and what the Buddha was, they do not at all agree with Zen's pretense to dislike all abstractions!

I believe there is a close relationship between Original Buddhism's Satipatthana Meditation (the Way of Mindfulness) and Zen training, however. So-called "Twenty-four-hour Zen" may well be the outcome of continued training in the Satipatthana. Where I have taught "Comparative Meditation," I have been pleased to note how people take to the profound Satipatthana practice (very positive, not at all passive like some of the Indian meditations) and how the discipline has begun to permeate every aspect of their everyday lives. This is real progress. When we buy books of clever words, memorize aphorisms, and attend courses that consist of our passively listening, we may feel good, but we make no headway at all in changing ourselves. With practice of the Satipatthana, and with concentrated Zen practice, we certainly can make such change. We hear that Hakuin Zenji, the great Japanese Zen Master, after experiencing his enlightenment, stated, "After that, seeing things of the world was like looking at the back of my own hand." This helps us to understand the Buddhist saying "Not Two," but we can never know the Unity of All Life simply by reading such statements, no matter how true they seem to be.

The truth is that the scattered mind is Hell, and that the focused mind brings Bliss. Dogen Zenji told us that, without training, there is no enlightenment experience. Therefore, to expect to achieve the straightforward mind without effort (and, curiously, such a mind connotes "no effort") is not realistic.

Can we profit from Zen Meditation (and Zen practice) if we do not really wish for Ultimates but simply want to make the world a more joyous place in which to live? Perhaps we can take a little self-inventory in order to answer that question.

Do I bang doors shut, or do I close them quietly? When I walk from one room to another or close a cabinet door, do I do so effortlessly and without noise or do I unconsciously (and impatiently) slam things shut? This is an important question, and the answer will be self-revealing. Actually, to slam a door is felt to "lose face" in much of the Far East.

When we have nothing in particular to do, do we sit quietly or do we leaf through magazines, turn on the radio or television in order to have some chatter to drown out our thoughts, or get up and pace around? How many of us sit still, in strong awareness, at such a time, without feeling compelled to "do something"?

In the bathroom, do we use great quantities of water, needlessly, or are we frugal? Dogen Zenji, when he scooped water from the stream near Eihei-ji, always returned half a dipperful to the stream. In washing, Zen aspirants are very economical in the amount of water they use, and this includes the important act of washing the feet.

Dogen insisted that kitchen workers refer to the items of food, such as rice, by their "honorable" names. Do we have respect for the things that feed us and that sacrifice their lives to do so? Or do we take such matters for granted? In fact, do we feel gratitude every day, rain or shine? The happy person is a compassionate one who is overwhelmed with gratitude. Zen writer Paul Reps once wrote, "How grateful I am with no-thing to be grateful for."

Let's examine our posture. Do we slump, lean forward as we walk, sit in a semi-reclining manner, or convey our dissatisfaction in the way we stand? Are we even conscious of our posture, which tells so much to the observing eye of a true teacher?

And lastly, do we lead more and more artificial lives? When it is a little colder, do we adjust the climate to ourselves by putting on the heat or insist on air-conditioning as soon as it becomes slightly warm? I once heard a Japanese scholar lecture some westerners, including myself, on this matter, saying that the Oriental adjusts him or herself to the environment, while Americans and Europeans attempt to change the environment to suit themselves. From the time of Imperial Rome until the present, we have attempted to "conquer" and control nature. The Japanese traditionally attempt to blend in with nature, and the Chinese believe in flowing with the Tao. Do we live on headache powders, stimulants, ethical drugs of all sorts (which were the beginning of a "drug culture"), and drink and smoke without really enjoying both activities? Are we irritable and do we think of all the world as "self-seeking"? And do we realize such self-seeking is the first step that leads to ruinous competition and to wars? When we are quarrelsome, do we always cite the other as being to blame for our irritation (which may have nothing to do with the other), thus rationalizing the chronic state of our own temperament and metabolism? *Why* don't we feel good, and *why* do we tend to be grouchy?

These questions are really outside the scope of this book, but they may cause the reader to introspect for a minute or two, thus serving a definite purpose. And if the results of introspection are to cause some dismay, then we may want to undertake Zen Meditation — and eventually Zen training — in order to change ourselves and, through ourselves, the world. No two of us see the same world as no two observers note the same scene; their eyes have different capabilities, and they have different levels of awareness. Therefore, we must work on the observer and leave the observed to itself. There is no doubt that what we observe will change as the observer changes. There are few ways in the world as effective as Zen training for bringing about such subjective change. And then, trying only to effect a more friendly world, we may have sudden insights that bring home the meaning of life and stir a religious gratitude in our hearts. Zen will then have given us a profound bonus! But that is part of the way of Zen Buddhism.

The Glossary that follows is fairly detailed, with much commentary that may be of interest to the serious reader. It is suggested that the reader take the time to read the Glossary to better understand much of what has been discussed in previous chapters.

Glossary — Commentary

ACUPUNCTURE — Ancient Chinese medicine involving use of needles, moxery (deep heat) and massage. It is said that acupuncture doctors take nine pulses and can make a diagnosis of the inner organs in this way. Using what it calls the "Meridian Channels," through which the Chi force flows, acupuncture is able to treat the inner organs through outer openings. Traditional Chinese medicine feels that illness is largely due to an imbalance of the "Yin" and "Yang" elements (Female and Male, Negative and Positive, Cold and Hot, etc.) and works to bring these back into balance. Traditionally, acupuncture is said to go back thousands of years to the days of the legendary Yellow Emperor, Huang.

ALTAR SUTRA — Also known as "The Platform Sutra" and "The Scripture of the Sixth Patriarch." Though the word "Sutra" implies that the contents were actual words of Gautama Buddha, it is known that the "Altar Sutra" represents direct quotes from lectures given by Hui-neng, the Sixth Patriarch, to monks and lay people alike in the seventh century in China. It is a sign of great respect to the supposedly illiterate Hui-neng, sometimes called the founder of Modern Zen, that his spoken words, copied by one of his disciples, are accorded the status of Scripture.

AMIDA — Japanese name for Amitabha, the Buddha of Infinite Light. Shin Buddhism in Japan is often referred to as "The Amida Cult," and statues and pictures of this non-historic Buddha are plentiful in the Japanese islands.

AMITABHA — The name for the Buddha of Infinite Light in India and China, known as Amida in Japan. Not historical.

AN-ATMAN — In Sanskrit, the word "Atman" has, roughly, the connotation of Soul. The Atman is felt to be changeless and eternal, in essence, one with Brahman. An-Atman, the Buddhist doctrine, says there is no eternal Soul or substance and that what appears to be the self is merely the false result of the collection of Skandhas, the so-called "five heaps." This was, and is, a radical view in India, where the immutability of the Atman is established in other Scriptures, such as the Upanishads and the Bhagavaad Gita.

ANANDA — The Buddha's cousin and attendant, who did not reach his enlightenment until after the death of his Master. It is said that he performed the remarkable feat of remembering all the Buddha's addresses and later was able to repeat them, verbatim, at a council held to determine what was to be considered canon. These words were passed on verbally for about four hundred years before being committed to writing. These sermons are now referred to as "Sutras."

ANICCA — The doctrine of "impermanence." Buddha said that all things are constantly in a state of flux, not remaining unchanged even for a second. A realization of this Truth is necessary if one is to avoid suffering.

ARHAT — Also known as "Arhant," this refers to the completely-enlightened saint, free of all "outflows," who has entered Nirvana (Nirvana is not an after-death state but freedom from all conditioning). The Buddha is often called "The Great Arhat." This term is used in Hinayana, the so-called "Lesser Vehicle" Buddhism, where the goal is to work out one's own Salvation. It contrasts with the "Bodhisattva" of Mahayana ("Greater Vehicle") Buddhism, the enlightened one who forgoes his or her own Salvation in order to remain where there is suffering and who vows to save all sentient beings.

AVALOKITESVARA — Male in India, this great enlightened Bodhisattva became female in China and Japan where "she" is known as Kuan Yin and Kwannon, sometimes referenced as "The Goddess of Mercy." A compassionate heart is often referred to as "The Heart of Kwannon," who never judges but only succors and saves.

BASHO — Japan's most famous Haiku poet, who lived in Kyoto but continually walked around Japan to observe nature and exchange Haiku with others. It is known that he practiced Zen early in life.

BASSUI — A fourteenth century Japanese Zen Master, who lived a hermit existence for a long time before consenting to take disciples and teach.

BHAKTI — One of the four main types of Indian Yoga. Bhakti Yoga refers to the practice of devotion as the way, and devotees (called Bhaktas) usually are devoted to some personal aspect of Divinity, such as Rama, Krishna, Shiva, etc.

BODHIDHARMA — The First Chinese Patriarch. Bodhidharma is supposed to have been a high-caste Indian teacher who came to China in the sixth century. While Buddhism had arrived in China at least four centuries earlier, Bodhidharma, the "Wall-Gazing Brahmin," stressed meditation and Sutra study rather than philosophy. He supposedly had only three disciples, and it was the teaching of the Meditation sect (Zen, Ch'an) that he passed along to his successor, the Second Patriarch Hui-Ke. Bodhidharma did stress the message of the profound "Lankavatara Sutra" as representing his own views, so he was not unaware of Buddhist Scriptures. He also is credited with being one of the founders of the so-called

Chinese Martial Arts known as "shadow-boxing." It is
said that he taught a method of self-defense to the monks
of Shaolin Temple that did not require any weapons, and
this probably was the forerunner of Judo, Aikido, Karate
and self-defense aspects of T'ai Chi Ch'uan.

BODHISATTVA — "Bodhi" refers to Enlightenment, "Sat" can
mean Being, and the syllable "Tva" can be translated as
"The Essence of." This would make a Bodhisattva "The
Essence of an Enlightened Being." At any rate, there
were felt to be many stages of Bodhisattva-hood, culmi-
nating in one known as a "Maha Satva," a Bodhisattva
who had reached the highest level — the next step would
result in Buddhahood. In his great vows, the compassionate Bodhisattva renounces entrance into Nirvana so
that he or she can stick around in suffering Samsara to
save all sentient beings before that one, him or herself,
reaches final Salvation. The "Bodhisattva" is the ideal of
Mahayana Buddhism, just as the "Arhat" represents the
highest level of Hinayana Buddhism.

BUBBLING SPRING — Known as "Hsueh" in Chinese, this
refers to the sole of the foot, a key point in acupuncture
and a good place for Martial Arts students to concentrate.
T'ai Chi Ch'uan teachers say that the Chi Energy is
drawn up through the soles of the feet (Hseuh) and
distributed by the waist, which must be exceptionally
pliable.

BUDDHA — The word "Buddha" refers to a Perfect One, a Saint
who has gone beyond Bodhisattva-hood, ended all
"outflows," and become the All-Knowing and All-Seeing.
Though later schools stress the omniscience of Buddhas,
there is no thought that a Buddha is a Creator or a God.
While we know of only one man in historic times who
was referred to as Buddha — the Prince of the Sakya

Tribe, Gautama Siddhartha — legend says that there have been innumerable Buddhas in the past, with Gautama being the seventh in what might be called Our Period of Time. Of course, when we get into esoteric Tibetan teaching, the word "Buddha" has a different, and esoteric connotation, and Gautama was simply felt to be an historic manifestation of this Eternal Principle. (Usually Tibetan Buddhism speaks of five Buddhas as forming the principle, with Vairocana Buddha being the main One.) Gautama Buddha predicted that the next Historic Buddha would be Maitreya, who is now supposed to be in the Tushita Heaven. Some estimate that it will be another two thousand years before Maitreya appears on earth to re-establish Dharma, and his teaching will be the same as Gautama's. It is interesting that legendary Dipankara Buddha, aeons ago, predicted that the Bodhisattva he then met would one day be Gautama, known as Sakyamuni. It is also interesting to note that Hindus, quite separately, have spoken of a coming Avatar known as Maitreya.

BUDDHA NATURE — It is basic to Enlightenment of all schools of Buddhism that one comes to realize all beings have, or, more exactly, are Buddha Nature. In other words, in essence all are One. This is not something to be learned but simply to be realized. Perhaps the most famous of all Koans is the one where Chao Chou (Joshu) is asked whether a puppy has Buddha Nature. Dogen Zenji pointed out that this should read "*is* Buddha Nature" rather than "*has* Buddha Nature," which implies possession. After the Fifth Patriarch imparted the Transmission of Mind to him in the middle of the night, Hui-neng spontaneously struck off a Gatha that com mented on how marvelous and incomprehensible was the fact that all, alike, possessed the One True Nature.

BURMESE METHOD — There are many fine meditation academies in Burma that teach the highly-concentrated Vipassana exercise referred to as the "Burma Method." Bypassing Dhyana (traditional Meditation), a ten-day or two-week course requires that one follow certain concentrated practices of Mindfulness for twenty hours of each day, the objective being to force a Vipassana experience (like a small Satori). This Method is now taught in India (at Bombay and Bodhi Gaya) and in Ceylon (Sri Lanka), as well as in Burma, and is not unknown in Thailand. Many who have practiced this arduous Method claim to have experienced a "sudden insight."

BUSHINSHU — One great Japanese Zen Master insists that Bodhidharma never used the words "Ch'an" or "Zen," but referred to his practice as "Bushinshu," which points directly at the realization of Buddha Nature. It must then be assumed that Bodhidharma learned fluent Chinese — which, in any case, would have been necessary for his famous interview with the emperor.

CH'AN — The Chinese name for "Zen." Some teachers claim that the word "Ch'an" simply means "Mind" or "Seeing into one's Nature." However, etymologically, "Ch'anna" is the Chinese pronunciation (transliteration) of the Sanskrit "Dhyana" or the Pali "Jhana," probably the latter. Ch'an is short for "Ch'anna."

CHA-NO-YU — Traditional Japanese Tea Ceremony, brought from China by the Zen Master Eisai (who also brought over Rinzai Zen) and perfected by the famous Tea Master, Sen no Rikyu.

CHAO CHOU — The Chinese Zen Master known as "Joshu" in Japanese. Probably the last of the T'ang Dynasty great

Ch'an (Zen) teachers, Chao Chou is supposed to have begun formal study of Ch'an at the age of 60, reached enlightenment at 80, and then to have taught until he was 120 years of age. Many of the most famous Koans come from his lips, and one contemporary Zen Master referred to him reverently as "The Ancient Buddha of Chao Chou." (Zen Masters are usually named, by posterity, after the mountain on which they taught or the locality from which they came.)

CHELA — One of the words in India for a disciple, one who has been initiated by a Master who has become his Guru.

CHI — This word has many meanings in Chinese. In this instance, it refers to the "Vital Force," the Intrinsic Energy that flows through the Meridian Channels of the body. This Chi can be separated into "Yin Chi" and "Yang Chi," and the primary purpose of Chi Kung practices (such as T'ai Chi Ch'uan and T'ai Chi Chih) is to circulate and balance this Chi. It is known as "Ki" in Japanese and as "Prana," "Sakti," or "Kundalini" in Indian languages.

CHIH KUAN — The deceptively simple T'ien T'ai meditation, with "Chih" representing "fixation" or stopping and "Kuan" referring to a "view." The "fixation" means concentration on a point in the body (usually the spot below the navel, the tip of the nose or the place between the eyes. Sometimes, in what is called the "three heaters" in Chinese, the lower abdomen is used as a focus of concentration). The "view" means introspecting the thought to see where it comes from and where it goes. Chih Kuan can also be used for Healing Practices and, as taught in Chinese T'ien T'ai and Japanese Tendai, can become enormously profound, extending to every phase of consciousness.

CHUANG-TZU — The great Taoist, who is believed by some to have been the outstanding writing stylist in China's history, as well as one of her greatest philosophers. Much of what we know of Lao-Tzu's Taoism comes from the writing of the later Sage, Chuang-Tzu, and while the former may not truly be historical, there is no doubt of the historicity of Chuang-Tzu. His works were much admired by Chinese Ch'an Masters, and he was often quoted.

CYPRESS TREE IN THE GARDEN — This phrase refers to Chao Chou's (Joshu's) answer to a monk's question about the meaning of Buddhism (literally, the meaning of Bodhidharma's coming from the west). Some feel Chao Chou was gazing at a cypress tree at that moment. This answer is one of the most puzzling of Koans, and it is not often penetrated by relative beginners.

DAI SESSHIN — In Japan, this is usually referred to as "The Great Seven-Day Meditation Session." However, Rinzai Master Joshu Sasaki says that it means "Sesshin in Itself," with no Great involved. Also, this fine teacher points out that any coming-together for Zen Meditation (Zazen) is Sesshin.

DHARMA — When spelled with a capital "D" (Dharma), it usually means the "Teaching" or the "Way." The Buddhadharma would refer to the Buddha Way or Teaching of Buddhism. When spelled with a lower-case "d" (dharma), it refers to phenomena, what the Chinese acknowledge as "The Ten Thousand Things." It is important to know this difference or the reader (and student) will be greatly confused. "Dharma" in India usually refers to the ancient "Sanatana Way," the Pure (Sattvic) Way of Life. Dharma can also be translated as "Doctrine."

DHARMA-DECLINING AGE — The Buddha, before his ParaNirvana (death) prophesied that the true Buddha Dharma would last only about 500 years, followed by another thousand years of slow decline, and then by a long period in which few would live according to the Teaching (finally to disappear, until the next Buddha, Maitreya, made his appearance). So it is extremely rare in these times to find one who can follow the ancient ways. Shin Buddhism feels we of this age are too degenerate to reach salvation by our own efforts, and this somewhat corresponds to the teaching of Hinduism, which says that this is the Kali Yuga (Iron Age), the most degenerate of four long periods known as Yugas.

DHYANA — In Sanskrit this word means "Meditation," and is sometimes referred to as "Absorption" in Buddhist Scriptures. It is deeper than mere Concentration.

DHYANA ABSORPTIONS — The Buddhist Scriptures speak of Four Absorptions, that is, ever-deepening stages of Meditation. Really, at this point, the Absorptions refer to what traditional Indian sources call "Samadhi," though this term has a somewhat different connotation in Buddhism.

DHYANA WASSON — The "Song of Meditation," written by eighteenth century Zen Master Hakuin in Japan.

DIAMOND SUTRA — Known as the "Vajracchedika-Prajna-Paramita Sutra" or "The Diamond Cutter of Doubts." This Scripture, one of the favorites of Zen Masters, stresses that there really is no such entity, ego-center or life as we usually conceive, and is supposed to have been the Sutra that directly led to the Sixth Patriarch's Enlightenment. It is certainly one of the most influential of Mahayana Scriptures and very difficult for the uninitiated to understand. The Buddha himself granted that this, and such Declarations, would probably terrify the average person.

DOGEN — Dogen Zenji was the founder of Soto Zen in Japan, though he himself did not like to divide Buddhism into sects and did not use the word "Zen" at all. Born in 1200, he received the approval of Japanese Masters while still young but did not feel satisfied by their teaching. Finally, he made the difficult journey to China, where he studied many years under the Chinese Master, Ju-Ching. Receiving Inka (Final Approval) from this Master, Dogen came back to Japan with what he felt was the "True Transmission," only to run into great opposition from other schools of Buddhism around Kyoto. He finally retreated deep into the mountains, where his temple, Eihei-ji, became the Spiritual Center for the great Soto Zen sect in Japan. Although Dogen had been exposed to Koan practice in Japan and to esoteric teachings of the Ts'ao Tung sect in China, he felt that these both led to intellectualism and "dialectics" and stressed the practice of Zazen (the Shikan Taza method) in his writings. Those who have read Dogen's profound "Shobogenzo" consider him one of the greatest philosophers, if not the greatest, in Japan's history. Certainly he was one of the two most influential Zen Masters that Japan has known.

DRY DUNG — This answer was made to a monk by a Master when the Monk asked what the Buddha really was. It is, of course, iconoclastic, and would tend to take away any useless veneration of a Buddha figure, but as a Koan, it has a much deeper significance.

DUKKHA — In Sanskrit this word, the opposite of "Sukkha," means "Suffering." Used in the Buddhist sense, it goes far beyond the "pleasure-pain" syndrome and points to the suffering in being separated from our own True

Nature. "All beings suffer," said the Buddha, meaning any individualized life center. With humans, Greed, Anger, and Delusion lead inevitably to suffering.

EIHEI-JI — In the mountains northwest of Tokyo is the Eihei-ji, the temple of Dogen, which is the spiritual center of Japanese Soto Zen. The setting is still beautiful, the weather cool and the place a mecca for many adherents, but the routines have changed greatly from Dogen's day. The temple now accommodates as many as 300 overnight visitors at a time and has quite a bit of pageantry for their benefit.

EISAI — This Zen Master (1141-1195) brought Lin-Chi Zen to Japan, where it is known as "Rinzai Zen." He also brought the traditional Tea Ceremony from China. It is largely because of Eisai that Zen came to Japan, for this was its first appearance after other sects of Buddhism had prepared the way.

ENERGY SEA — This refers to the primordial Chi energy, that which Professor Wen-Shan Huang calls "The Chi a Priori," generally felt to have its source just below the navel (T'an T'ien in Chinese, Tanden in Japanese). Some dispute this, however, and feel the home of this timeless energy is elsewhere in the body. Hakuin refers to it often in his "Yasenkanna."

ENGO — A Chinese Zen Master mentioned in the classic Mumonkan, which discusses "Cases" (Koans) which the Master Mumon felt to be of special interest.

ENTERING THE STREAM — Buddhism feels that there is no effect without a cause. It speaks of "The Causal Ground" and "The Seed," meaning the seed of Buddha Nature. Once one has taken a step in the direction of the Buddhist Teaching — even if only to achieve some merit or some "blessing" from the giving of alms — it is felt that a seed has been sown and one has "entered the stream." Then it is only a matter of time until one begins to follow the Buddha Dharma. In effect, it means that a start toward spirituality has been made and one day must come to fruition.

ESSENTIAL NATURE — Each of us has his or her "Own True Nature," which is synonymous with the omnipresent Buddha Nature. To recognize our "Essential Nature" means to ignore the temporary aberrations of mind and personality, of world and phenomena, and perceive that which is lasting, that which acts through us.

FASTING MIND — An expression used by Chuang-Tzu to denote the mind that was ridding itself of the superficial. Most of us think of constantly adding to our knowledge (memorization of "facts"), but the Taoism for which Chuang-Tzu was such a great spokesperson constantly admonished "losing a little each day." The trend toward simplicity and naturalness which is inferred here is one that is greatly needed in the world of today.

FIVE HINDRANCES — The "five hindrances" to enlightenment are said to be: Anger, Sloth or Torpor, Agitation, Worry and Skepticism or Doubt. It is true that Zen expects one practicing the Koan to develop a "great doubt," but this is considerably different from the lack of confidence in the essential Buddha Nature. To practice Zen skeptically would be the opposite of "giving oneself" completely to the practice.

FIVE RANKS — Supposedly devised by Tung-Shan Liang-Chien (Tozan in Japanese), this is one of the most profound of all Zen "Koans" or Teaching. It is seldom taught in Japan today, and Dogen Zenji did not bring it back from China (where it was an essential part of the Ts'ao Tung sect) because he thought it would lead to "dialectics" and he preferred plain, unadulterated Zazen. "The Five Ranks" have to do with the juxtaposition of what has been called the "Apparent" and the "Real." The first two of the five difficult verses are titled: "The Apparent within the Real" and "The Real within the Apparent." Many Masters have spent years in trying to realize the true meaning of "The Five Ranks," even after their own Enlightenment.

FIXATION — The Chinese have usually believed that meditation, to be successful, demands concentration on some point of the body, such as the space between the eyes, the tip of the nose, or the spot below the navel. Such concentration tends to keep away all other thoughts. Depending on which spot is chosen for Fixation, there are apt to be varied physical effects.

FOUR-CORNERED NEGATION — The basis of the "Middle Way" in Buddhism, this refers to the continued negative way (via negativa) which denies "is," "is not," "both is and is not" and "neither is nor is not," thus wiping out all logical categories, opening a way for the realization of the Absolute, which certainly cannot be subsumed under any category.

FOUR VOWS — These are taken by the Bodhisattva, or the true student of Mahayana, essentially promising to overcome the passions, enter all Dharma doors, fulfill the Buddha Way, and save all sentient beings before oneself. It is important that the one chanting these vows in combination Chinese-Japanese knows the meaning of the solemn promises he or she is making.

FRUITS OF KARMA — Karma means "Action" in Sanskrit. Each action (and this includes thought or intent) must result in an equal reaction. Thus, "as we sow, so shall we reap." "The fruit of our actions" is our own personal destiny, carried on through many lives.

GASSHO — When a Buddhist brings the two palms of the hands together in front of the chest in an attitude that resembles prayer, he or she is making a "Gassho," a gesture that conveys respect in Buddhism, somewhat like the pranam used in India. It does not indicate "prayer." One Soto Zen teacher says that, in the Gassho, the left hand signifies "the world" and the right hand "Reality."

GATHA — A verse, usually spontaneous and four lines in length, in the classic Chinese style, spoken by a Zen person, reflecting one's realization. In the so-called "Zen Sickness," an enlightened monk might continually spout such pronouncements without any willful effort on his part. The great gathas of the Zen patriarchs, particularly their last statements, have been carefully preserved through the long history of Zen in India, China, and Japan. (Some scholars feel that the gathas of Indian patriarchs are apocryphal and were composed much later than is commonly believed.)

GAUTAMA — Gautama Siddhartha was the name of the Indian Prince who later came to be known as Buddha. His tribe's name was "Sakya," and he is also known as "Sakyamuni."

GENJO KOAN — Defined as "Accomplished in the Present," meaning our life and our world, just as they are now, are right. This means recognition and acceptance of "what is," as opposed to interminable planning for "what might be," an absolute necessity for living in the present. The Genjo Koan is the property of the Soto Zen sect, and I have not heard this term used in Rinzai.

GOLDEN AGE OF ZEN — The T'ang Dynasty (618-906?) is often called the Golden Age of Zen in China. From the time of Hui-neng (638-713?) until the passing of Chao Chou (died about 898), there was a great surge of vitality in China. It is felt that, for a while, there were over one million monks! This was the period when the five great Schools of Zen developed, and numerous great Ch'an Masters made their appearance. All were lineal descendants of the "illiterate" Hui-neng, who certainly fathered all modern Zen.

GOLDEN PAVILION — Known as Kinkaku-ji in Japanese, this famous temple building burned down completely in the past and was built again to the exact same specifications. Present-day Japanese feel it is still too new and gaudy for their taste, but it is certainly one of the most photographed structures in Japan, being in the northern part of the city of Kyoto.

GREAT CIRCLE MEDITATION — My own name for a Meditation I developed from some of the practices of Taoism (described and taught in detail in the author's book *T'ai Chi Chih/Joy thru Movement*). It has been my experience, as teacher, that this Meditation seems to fit almost any temperament and seems to afford healing and energizing results. It is called "Great Circle" because it involves taking "The True Thought" — actually, the flowing Chi — in a complete circle of the torso.

HAKUIN — One of the two greatest influences in the Japanese history of Zen, this Rinzai Master (1685-1768) revived the dying Zen in Japan, and all lines of Rinzai Masters come through him. He seems to have been very aware of Taoist practices and writes about same in his unusual "Yasenkanna," calling them "The True Zen." Despite his recommendation, these practices seem to have largely disappeared in Japan.

Hakuin introduced many Koans in Japan, perhaps the only Japanese Zen Master to do so. For instance, the "One Hand Sound" Koan is said to be his. After his Enlightenment (he had had a partial Satori at an earlier time, but the Masters of that era refused to confirm it), he supposedly made the statement that: "After this Realization, seeing the things of the world was like looking at the back of my own hand. Only then could I understand how it is the Buddha-Eye which sees the Buddha-Nature." It is interesting that, even after his Enlightenment, Hakuin had great trouble in understanding "The Five Ranks," (described above) which gives one an idea of the complexity of that teaching or Koan. Hakuin's poverty-stricken mountain temple, called Shoju-an (after his teacher, Shoju), is still standing and active in the northern mountains of the island of Honshu.

HAKUYU — The Mountain Hermit (Sennin), supposedly of great age, who taught Hakuin the "Nai Kan," or "Inner Contemplation." He was called by Hakuin the "Perfect Man."

HALF-LOTUS — This is the Meditation position where one sits with one leg up on the opposite thigh, as opposed to the "Full Lotus," where both legs are placed, soles up, on the opposite thighs.

HALL OF JADE — The way the Taoists refer to the important spot between the eyes, often called "The Third Eye" in occult literature.

HEART SUTRA — Known as the "Shin Gyo" in Chinese, or "Maka Hanya Haramita Shin Gyo" ("The Heart Sutra of the Prajnaparamita," or Perfection of Wisdom), this Sutra was originally called "Hridaya" (Heart Sutra) in Sanskrit. It is felt to delineate the "heart" or kernel of the great Prajnaparamita teaching, being the gist of all that is in the more than 1600 Prajnaparamita Sutras. Prajnaparamita is sometimes personalized in Buddhism, and then is called "The Mother of All Buddhas," but generally, it is defined according to the words "Paramita" (meaning "Perfection") and "Prajna" (meaning "Wisdom"). Some have also loosely described Prajnaparamita as "That which takes one to the Other Shore," meaning "The Way to Nirvana."

HIEI — A famous mountain near Kyoto with a famous and ancient Buddhist monastery on top.

HINAYANA — Original Buddhism, known as "The Lesser Vehicle" by some. (Hinayanists, quite understandably, prefer to refer to themselves under the heading "Theravada," or "The Way of the Elders.") Mahayana Buddhism (The Greater Vehicle) is more widespread in the Far East than Hinayana, which continues strong in Ceylon (Sri Lanka), Burma, and Thailand.

HOGEN ZEN — The Japanese name for the Fa-yen sect in China. This was one of the more philosophic and intellectual Zen schools (one of the "Big Five"), and it disappeared in both China and Japan. It is felt that it has been assimilated by the Lin-Chi (or Rinzai) school, but the keen insights of its founder are admired and frequently studied by all Zen people.

HONEN — Son of a Samurai family, Honen became the founder of "Jodo" in Japan (the so-called "Amida Cult") and was the teacher of Shinran, who founded the great Jodo Shinshu sect. Supposedly, Honen became a monk on the admonition of his dying father, rather than following tradition and seeking revenge on his father's slayer. Honen-In (down the road on the famous "Philosopher's Walk," a bit from Ginkakuji, the Silver Pavilion, in the eastern part of Kyoto), is one of my favorite temples in

Japan, though not large and not well-patronized by tourists. There is a large figure of Amida Buddha there, visible only on certain special holidays.

HSIN — "Kokoro" in Japanese, means "Heart-Mind-Spirit" in Chinese.

HUA-T'OU — One Chinese scholar has defined the Hua-T'ou as "that which is antecedent to thought," meaning the mind in its pure condition between thoughts (what Indian philosophy would refer to as the Turiya State). Actually, the Hua-T'ou in operation is that part of a Koan with which the student grapples — for instance, "Mu" in Chao Chou's Koan about whether a puppy has Buddha Nature.

HUAI-JANG — A direct Spiritual Descendant of Hui-neng, Huai-jang became the Master of Ma-Tsu, one of the most influential of all Chinese Zen Masters (often known as "The Horse-Master," as the word "Ma" means "Horse" in Chinese, and "Tzu" refers to a Master or Sage).

HUI-NENG (638-713) — Became the Sixth and last Patriarch of Chinese Zen, but he actually was the Father of Modern Zen. Before his time, Zen (and other Buddhist practice in China) simply continued Indian tradition, relying heavily on translations of Indian Sutras and on practice of Indian-style Meditation. Hui-neng changed all that and really originated the School of "Instantaneous Enlightenment," as well as emphasizing that it was the great "Prajna Wisdom," natural to all, that was important, rather than mere quiet sitting-in-meditation. Northern Zen, as opposed to his Southern School, continued to be quietistic in practice even after Hui-neng began to teach, but after Hui-neng's death, his disciple Shen-hui success-fully guided his Master's school to ascendancy over the Northern Zen of Shen-Hsiu, and the latter eventually died completely. Hui-neng is said to have produced over

forty enlightened disciples — an extraordinary number —
and from these pupils and their disciples came the five
great Schools of Chinese Zen, the Kuei-Yang (Ikyo) sect,
the Lin-Chi (Rinzai) sect, the Yun-Men (Ummon) sect,
the Fa-Yen (Hogen) sect and the Ts'ao Tung (Soto) sect.
The story of Hui-neng ("Wei Lang," "Eno" in Japanese) is well-known. An illiterate seller of firewood who
lived with his widowed mother, the young man chanced
to hear someone reciting the "Diamond Sutra," and he
instantaneously grasped its import. Providentially, an
acquaintance gave him some gold coins to support his
mother so he could make the long trip to meet the Fifth
Zen Patriarch, Hung-jen, who expounded this sutra. Hui-
neng was treated as a "barbarian" when he arrived at
Hung-jen's monastery, but the latter must have been
deeply impressed by the young man's statement: "I
confess to Your Reverence that I feel Wisdom constantly
springing from my own heart and mind. So long as I do
not stray from my nature, I carry within me the Field of
Bliss."* This, of course, graphically conveys the heart of
Hui-neng's own teaching, which was to revolutionize
Zen.

   After being a humble rice-pounder for about eight
months, during which time he had no contact with the
Master, Hui-neng became aware of the gatha that the
Head Monk, Shen-hsiu, had written for the Master, and
Hui-neng answered with his own four-line stanza. Being
illiterate, someone had to write it for him. From these
two gathas Hung-jen was able to ascertain that the Head
Monk had not yet realized his Buddha Nature, but the

*Hui-neng's words quoted from *The Golden Age of Zen* by Dr.
John Wu.

rice-pounder undoubtedly had. Then, expounding the "Diamond Sutra" to Hui-neng in the middle of the night, the Fifth Patriarch took the extraordinary step of transferring the robe and bowl (symbols of the Zen patriarchs) to this illiterate man in his young twenties, who was not even a monk! Hui-neng then stayed under cover for a number of years, finally emerging to visit a temple, where he heard two resident monks arguing over whether the flag was moving or the wind was moving. "It is Mind that is moving!" asserted Hui-neng, and this unusual answer aroused the interest of the Abbot of that temple, who then confirmed that Hui-neng was the missing Sixth Patriarch. He shaved Hui-neng's head, imparted the Precepts to him and then became his disciple. The story of what followed and the heart of Hui-neng's "new" teaching, may be read in "The Altar Sutra" of the Sixth Patriarch, Hui-neng's sermons to great numbers of lay people and monks alike. It is strongly suggested that every Zen student read this Sutra many times.

I CHIN(G) — Means "Great Doubt," which the one using the Koan practice tries to produce. It is said that, "The greater the doubt, the bigger the Buddha!"

INDIAN YOGA — Yoga is, of course, the Science of Union, but there are many different kinds of Yoga in India. China, too, had its Yoga, which was Taoist in character.

INKA — It is said that there has been a "Direct Transmission of Mind" from the Buddha down to the present, and the practice of giving Inka preserves this heritage. When a Master gave Inka to his disciple, it meant complete approval of the latter's Enlightenment and permission for the disciple to teach and carry on the Master's tradition. Inka has never been given lightly, and usually not quickly, though Hui-neng did give Inka to the remarkable Yung-Chia on the latter's first visit to him, after which Yung-Chia was known as "The Overnight Enlightened One." Many monks have taught without Inka, but this was without full approval of their Masters.

INTRINSIC ENERGY — The "Chi a Priori" that is with anyone from the time he or she is born. This somewhat corresponds to Zen's "Your Original Face" and is felt by most to be similar to "The Vital Force," often known as Prana. I urge all Zen students to cultivate this energy. My experience with T'ai Chi Chih has shown me the value of such effort.

INZO — The technical name for the hand position (Mudra) in Zazen.

JAPA — Repetition of a Mantra (name of God or Sacred Word or Phrase), either orally, mentally, or by being half-muttered. In Likita Japa, one writes the Mantra a prescribed number of times. Mental (Manasika) Japa is the same as Transcendental Meditation. The purpose of Japa is to steady the mind; when it becomes one-pointed, Japa with the eyes closed turns into "Deep Meditation."

JHANA — The Pali word for Meditation, same as "Dhyana" in Sanskrit.

JODO SHINSHU — The new school of Jodo ("The Amida Cult") in Japan, founded by Shinran. It is probably the largest sect of Buddhism in Japan, unless one considers Soka Gakkai a true Buddhist sect. Constant repetition of "Namu Amida Butsu" — "Hail to the Buddha of Infinite Light" — is the sole practice of the Jodo Shinshu adherent.

JU-CHING (1163-1228) — The Chinese Master of Dogen Zenji, a strict disciplinarian who, if we can believe Dogen's

account, was, nevertheless, greatly loved by his follow
ers.

KAKEMONO — A Hanging Scroll in Japan.

KALPA — An almost inconceivably long period of time,
composed of four so-called "Yugas," at the end of which,
according to East Indian thought, the Cosmos is con-
sumed in flame. There then remains only the potential
of the habit-energies of those who have lived, and from
these comes the next "Creation." The Buddha said to his
faithful attendant, Ananda, that a Buddha could, if he
wished, remain in his body until the end of his Kalpa.
Time, in India and in Buddhism, is thought of cyclically,
not as something that stretches out from beginning to end
in a linear fashion. Some have guessed that a Kalpa
lasts at least several million years.

KARASUMA — A major thoroughfare in Kyoto, Japan, the one
that runs by the ancient Emperor's Palace. (It goes from
north to south.)

KARMA — Literally means "Action" in Indian languages but is
often used instead of "Fruits of Karma" to mean the
destiny that one has created by one's own actions. "As
you sow, so shall you reap" is a good description of
Karma.

KEGON — The Japanese name for a highly-philosophical school
of Buddhism that stresses Negation as the path to
Reality, the final Negation being the negating of Negation itself.

KI — The Japanese equivalent of "Chi" in Chinese and "Prana"
in Sanskrit. It is the intrinsic energy of all life. Sometimes, in disciplines such as Aikido (the "Ki" syllable
referring to this energy), the Tanden, spot two inches
below the navel, is referred to as the "Ki."

KINHIN — The walking interval between periods of sitting Zazen. It is felt to be a continuation of the Meditation, while affording some much-needed exercise after long periods of sitting in meditation pose.

KOAN — "Kung-an" in Chinese, it literally means "a case," as in a law case. In Zen it refers to historic exchanges between Zen people. The final phrase in such an exchange is given to a Zen student as his or her special "problem." The student works with the Koan incessantly and meets with his or her Master in Sanzen (personal private confrontation) to offer a solution (not necessarily verbal) to the Koan. "Passing a Koan," that is, satisfying the Master with one's response, is a great moment in Rinzai Zen practice, and it sometimes takes years.

KUAN-YIN — Often called the "Goddess of Mercy," this female Bodhisattva (known as "Kwannon" in Japan) was the male Avalokitesvara in India. According to the "Surangama Sutra," he reached his great enlightenment by turning inward the organ of sound, the hearing faculty. Manjusri told the Buddha that this method of Avalokitesvara's was the one best suited to the ordinary person in the Dharma-Declining period. Kuan-Yin in China, and Kwannon in Japan are much beloved by the populace, and statues often show them with many arms so as to carry out the saving function.

KWANNON — Japanese name for Kuan-Yin.

KYOSAKU — The stick that is carried by a monk as he patrols the aisles in formal Zazen periods at Zendos and Temples. He is authorized to use it — usually with two blows on the right side of the neck and two on the left — when he comes on someone sitting badly or one whose mind is wandering. Being hit by the kyosaku is not a punishment but an aid in sitting.

KYOTO — The "Western Capitol," Kyoto became the capitol city
of Japan after Nara, less than one thousand years ago. It
continued as the capitol for the impotent emperor long
after the Shogun began to rule Japan from Edo, now
known as Tokyo. Kyoto, of course, is no longer the
capitol of the island (Tokyo is), though it is the traditional and cultural capitol of Japan in the minds of many.
So valuable were the art and religious treasures of Kyoto
felt to be that the city was never bombed by the United
States in World War II. There are about 1600 Buddhist
Temples in and around Kyoto, as well as many Shrines
and famous gardens. It is now a city of almost 1½
million inhabitants.

LIN-CHI — Lin-Chi Hsuan ("Rinzai" in Japanese, died about
866) was the disciple of the great Huang-po, and went on
to surpass his Master by creating a School of Ch'an
Buddhism that later assimilated most of the other Zen
Schools in China. The Koan device, used by all schools
at one time or another, is associated with Lin-Chi's way
of teaching, as is the use of various types of shouts.

The story of Lin-Chi's Enlightenment is well-known.
He had been a quiet, pious monk in Huang-po's monastery for about three years when the leader of the monks'
community, a fine man named Mu-chow Tao-ming,
suggested that he ask Huang-po about the essential
meaning of Buddhism. When he did so, Huang-po
repeatedly struck him with the hossu, or staff, that most
Zen Masters carry. Three times Lin-Chi went to his
Master's room to ask, and three times he was grossly
struck. Not understanding the significance, Lin-Chi
sadly decided to leave the monastery, at which time
Huang-po suggested that he walk down the river a bit to
visit the Ch'an Master, Ta-yu, who would explain the

whole incident. This Lin-Chi did, and was almost immediately enlightened, following which he came back to his Master, Huang-po.

In later years, Lin-Chi became one of the most dynamic of all Zen Masters, and certainly one of the most influential. He is well-remembered (and sometimes misunderstood) for his admonition: "When you meet a Buddha, kill the Buddha! If you encounter a Patriarch, kill him! Meeting an Arhat, strike him down! When you meet your mother and father, kill them too!" This terribly blood-thirsty statement is not to be taken literally, of course, breaking, as it does, many of the most sacred precepts of the religion. Rather, it was a call not to let any attachment stand in the way of Salvation — much like the act of Nan-ch'uan (Nansen) in cutting the cat in half. Lin-Chi also spoke of "The True Man of No Title," pointing at the Buddha Nature, and, curiously, added that "it" was coming in and out of the forehead all day long! Those who have practiced Chi Kung exercises know the significance of the third eye spot in the forehead, and this strongly indicates that Lin-Chi, like so many other Chinese Masters, was well aware of Taoist practices. Though the Japanese Master Hakuin also knew such practices, they seem to have faded out entirely in the Japanese Zen community.

Lin-Chi's influence is very much alive in the Zen world of today and is beginning to be felt in the West. He certainly was one of the three or four most important Masters in Zen and Ch'an history.

LOTUS POSTURE — The "Full Lotus" position in Yoga and Zen practice requires putting both feet up on the opposite thighs as one sits cross-legged.

LOTUS SUTRA — "Saddharma Pundarika," one of the most influential of all Buddhist Scriptures. Widely admired by Zennists, it is the very basis of study and practice for all the various Nichiren sects in Japan and elsewhere.

MA-TSU — Later known as "The Horse-Master" because his own surname, Ma, means "horse," and the Tsu (Sage or Master) was added as a measure of respect despite the fact that, after Hui-neng, there were to be no more patriarchs in Zen. Some feel that Ma-Tsu's influence on the history of Zen was second only to that of Hui-neng because of the great number of enlightened teachers turned out by the "Horse-Master." He received his Enlightenment at the hands of Huai-jang, and among his most celebrated disciples were Pai-chang (responsible for the code that governs Ch'an and Zen Monasteries) and Nan-ch'uan. The probable dates of Ma-Tsu's birth and death are 709-788.

MAHAYANA — Buddhism divided into two parts, much as Christianity did with Catholicism and Protestantism. The more modern of these divisions is the Mahayana (so-called "Greater Vehicle"), which offers the Bodhisattva, who vows to save all sentient beings, in contrast to the Hinayana Arhat, who is seeking his or her own Salvation. Hinayana followers feel that their way more closely approximates the original way of the Buddha. Zen is part of Mahayana Buddhism and often refers to Hinayana in a slightly disparaging manner.

MAKYO — One sitting long hours of Zazen may begin to hallucinate with the eyes wide open. Such visions or apparitions, pleasant or otherwise, are considered "Makyo," and the sitter is admonished to pay no attention to these creations of his or her own mind.

MANNA — Primitive tribes spoke of something mysteriously coming their way as "Manna from Heaven." It is a belief in supernatural grace and the gifts that result from it.

MAYA — The realm of Illusion. "Maya" and "Samsara" have roughly the same meaning.

MIAJIMA — A favorite tourist place of interest on the Inland Sea in Japan. There is a well-known Shinto Shrine there, and the red gate rising out of the water is one of the most photographed sights in Japan.

MIDDLE WAY — The "Madhyamika" of the great teacher, Nagarjuna, sometimes known as "The New Wisdom School." The Middle Way does not mean compromise but looks to the Mean as it denies all concepts in the four-cornered negation. Madhyamika exponents always pointed strongly at the Great Void as being the Truth of Buddhism.

MIND-ONLY — The Yogacara School of Buddhism believed there is nothing but Mind (Mere Ideation).

MONDO — A dialogue between two Zen people, usually between a Master and a Disciple. Often these Mondo became Koans.

MU — Koan, or hua-t'ou, used by a great many Zen students. It is the Chinese "Wu," meaning "no thing" or negative, the answer given by Zen Master Chao Chou (Joshu) to the monk who asked him if a dog had Buddha Nature.

MU-CHI — A Chinese monk-artist, known as "Mokke" in Japan and famous for such black-and white pictures as "The Six Persimmons," now in a temple in Japan. Perhaps no artist has better captured the feeling of "Suchness" that Zen people admire so much in painting.

MUDRA — Generally, the position of the hands is what Mudra means, as in classical Indian dancing or meditation postures, but Mudra really refers to the position and carriage of the whole body. It is said that a Zen Master can easily read a newcomer's state of mind from his or her bodily carriage.

MUSASHI — Miyamoto Musashi was a Samurai, the greatest swordsman in Japan's history. He received Zen training, and his comparatively simply pen-and-ink (Sumi-e) drawings are greatly admired by Zennists.

MUSHI BOSHI — The day on which Japanese temples bring out all their books and art treasures and air them out. It was on such a day that Hakuin aimlessly opened a book lying on the grass and received life-long inspiration from reading how the Abbot Jimyo, in order to stay awake during long hours of meditation, drove a gimlet into his thigh so the pain would heighten his awareness.

NAI KAN — The "Inner Contemplation" which Hakuin learned from the Mountain Hermit, Hakuyu. It enabled Hakuin to heal himself of his great illness. Actually, it is taken from a Taoist discipline and is one of the Chi Kung practices in China, where it is known as Nei Kung. (Instruction in this esoteric practice can be found in the author's book *Meditation for Healing/Particular Meditations for Particular Results.*)

NAMU MYOHO RENGE KYO — A phrase from the "Lotus Sutra" that is used by all Nichiren sects in Japan, as well as by some of the "new religions," for chanting. It works much like a Mantra.

NANSEN — Nan-ch'uan in Chinese. He was the pupil of Ma-tsu and became the Master of Chao Chou. A great teacher, he is perhaps best known for his incredible act of cutting the cat in half when he found two groups of monks squabbling over it, after first giving them a chance to

save the cat's life if "they could say a word of Zen."
(They couldn't.)

NARA — A small Kansai district city that was the original
capitol of Japan.

NEI KUNG — Same as the Japanese "Nai Kan," a way to
mentally start the Chi energy flowing from below the
navel to the soles of the feet. Considered by Chinese to
have great healing value.

NEMBUTSU — The "Namu Amida Butsu" (Hail to the Buddha
of Infinite Light) chanted by all Shin Buddhists, in the
firm belief that it will enable Amida Buddha to take the
believer to the "Western Paradise," the so-called "Pure
Land," where conditions will be ideal for attaining
Enlightenment.

NETI NETI — Means "Not this, not that," in Indian languages,
a way to Reality.

NIPPON — Also "Nihon," the Japanese people's own name for
Japan. It can mean "The Origin of the Sun."

NIRVANA — Literally, it means "Extinction" in Indian lan
guages and refers to the extinction of the "outflows," the
attachments and desires that keep one anchored in
suffering Samsara. Nirvana is not a Paradise; it is the
unconditioned state of Freedom. Unlike Hinayanists,
Mahayana people, and particularly Zennists, believe that
Nirvana and Samsara are the same, only cognized
differently.

OBAKU — Japanese name for Ch'an Master Huang-po, who was
the teacher of Lin-Chi (Rinzai). There is a Zen sect in
Japan named after Obaku. It has a famous temple in Uji
and uses the Nembutsu of Shin Buddhism as well as
some Shinto practices.

ORIGINAL FACE — A phrase often used by Zen Masters.
When Hui-neng was fleeing after receiving the robe and

bowl from his Master (at the age of 23), he was over-taken by a pursuer, to whom he gave his first instruction. He said, "Thinking neither of good nor bad, what is your Original Face before you were born?" It is said that Hui-ming, who had followed Hui-neng with evil intent, was instantaneously enlightened by this phrase and remarked that he was like a drinker who, alone, knew if the water was cold or hot. After all externals and all temporal things are discarded, what is left is one's "Original Face." "Show me your 'Original Face' before you were born," is a frequent command given by Masters to their pupils; it means for them to reveal their "True Nature."

OTHER POWER — Zen is a "Self-Power" path of Buddhism, as one depends on one's own efforts, while Christianity and Shin Buddhism would be "Other Power" paths, as they do not depend on one's own efforts but on one's surrender to a Greater Power.

OTHER-WORLDLY — Transcendent beliefs and practices which take one away from the everyday world are often called "Other-Worldly." Zen believes in being here now, that this world *is* the Other World, and so Zen is just the opposite of "Other-Worldly." Sometimes "Other-World-ly" ways of thought lead to a dreaminess and escapism.

PALI — Most of the early Sutras of Buddhism, those studied by Hinayanists, are in the Indian language of Pali, which superficially resembles Sanskrit. Theravada Buddhism generally studies only the so-called "Pali Canon."

POWERS — Known as "Siddhi" in Indian tongues, the term refers to the so-called "supernatural" powers that great austerity leads to in India. Zen teachers pay no attention to such phenomena, though in the long history of Zen, Masters have frequently demonstrated such ability. (For

example, Zen Masters have usually predicted the time
and circumstances of their own deaths.)

PRAJNA — Means "Wisdom." It is not acquired knowledge, but
the natural Wisdom of the mind. When the impurities of
mind are dissolved, when it rests in its own natural state,
the "Prajna Wisdom" shines of its own accord and
actions that arise from it are inevitably "right." This was
the basis of Hui-neng's teaching.

PRAJNAPARAMITA — Also known as "The Perfection of
Wisdom." Prajnaparamita, while sometimes personalized
as "The Mother of All Buddhas" by Mahayana Buddhism, generally refers to the more than 1600 Sutras that
expound "The Perfection of Wisdom." Transliterated by
the Chinese, this was called the Maka (from Sanskrit
"Maha," meaning "Great") Hanya Haramita.

PRANA — Indian teaching says that there are only two things in
the Universe, in the final analysis — Akasha (Space) and
Prana (Energy). Modern science seems to support this
view. Prana, all the energy of the Cosmos, is felt as a
circulating power in the body ("Chi" in Chinese, "Ki" in
Japanese), and in one of his most famous commentaries,
the Indian Sage Shankara says that this is the only Real.
Prana is synonymous with Shakti (the manifested power
of Shiva) and Kundalini. Some Indian philosophers refer
to different kinds of Prana (such as Apana, etc.). Certain
Indian and Chinese Taoist schools feel that mastery of
this Prana is the most important practice of all. In Tibet,
it is one of the disciplines that leads to creation of the
so-called "Inner Heat" (Dumo).

PRANAYAMIC — Refers to the Indian practice of "Pranayama,"
mastery of the breath or prana.

PURE LAND — Shin Buddhists of Japan are known as members
of the "Pure Land" sect, the Pure Land being the West-

ern Paradise where true believers will be taken by the Buddha of Infinite Light (Amida). Zen Masters often used this phrase in a different way, to mean the pure and straightforward mind.

QUIESCENCE — Much of Taoism and early Buddhism in China was quietist in nature, aiming, through silent meditation, to reach a state of Purity in the traditional Indian fashion. From Hui-neng's time on, such quiet practice was not the mainstay of Zen, and after Pai-Chang, who codified monastery rules for the Zen Buddhist community (Sangha), Zen monks were expected to work in the fields, a radical departure from Indian yogic tradition. Quiescence tends toward "Other-Worldliness," and this is not the way of Zen, where Nirvana is to be found right in this suffering Samsara.

RAJA YOGA — The eight-step Yogic Path codified and explained by the great Indian, Patanjali (the steps being: Yama, Niyama, Asana, Pranayama, Pratyahara, Concentration, Dhyana, Samadhi). This "Kingly" Yoga relies heavily on meditative practice and is said to produce great Powers or "Siddhi." It is one of the four main Yogas of India, the other three being Bhakti Yoga, Karma Yoga, and Jnana Yoga. All four use the Samkhya Cosmology as the basis for their philosophy.

RAMANA MAHARSHI — The great Gnani, teacher Advaita (Non-Duality), who died less than forty years ago. His Ashram at Tiruvanamali, with the famous Arunachala hill behind it, still continues. The Maharshi was one of the few Masters in Indian history who reached Enlightenment by himself, without a Guru, and he never referred to anybody as his disciple, as that would have been a duality in itself. Many have been interested in the discipline the Maharshi advised, the Maha Yoga that consisted of asking oneself, "Who am I?" to be followed by similar inquiries to determine who was the real do-er — much in the same way that Bassui wanted his followers to find who was the real "boss." It is my own opinion that everything the Maharshi believed and taught was compatible with, though highly different in language, from the teaching of Gautama Buddha. Certainly he was one of the greatest Sages in India's long history, and many books have been written about him.

RINZAI ZEN — Lin-Chi was the ninth century Zen Master who founded the Lin-Chi school of Zen, one of the Big Five divisions of Chinese Ch'an. The Japanese reading of his name is "Rinzai," and the Rinzai school is one of the two dominant divisions of Japanese Zen, specializing in Koan training as opposed to the "sitting-only" (Shikan-Taza) of Japanese Soto Zen. Though Eisai, in the twelfth century, brought Rinzai Zen to Japan, the eighteenth century Master, Hakuin Zenji, is looked upon as its great figure. He revived the school in the eighteenth century, contributed many of its most effective Koans, and became the source from which all Rinzai teachers have sprung.

RYOANJI — A Zen temple in Kyoto. It is famous for the unusual dry stone garden that has been much photographed. There seem to be no monks meditating at Ryoanji these days, but there are innumerable tourists (including groups of school children) visiting every day, paying an entrance fee to look at the world-famous garden, which contains no green. Known as "The Garden of the Slumbering Dragon," Ryoanji is usually considered a fifteenth century development.

RYOKAN — A wandering Zen monk in Japan, much beloved of children, who was particularly noted for his calligraphy. Though Ryokan was penniless most of his life, samples of his writing bring large sums of money. He was also noted as a poet, and there are collections of his appealing poetry in English.

SAIHO-JI — Popularly known as "Kokadera" (The Moss Garden Temple), this lovely Kyoto temple, built before the fourteenth century, is famous for the more-than-40 types of moss found on the rocks and grasses. It is located in the extreme western part of Kyoto.

SAKYAMUNI — The "Sakya" refers to the Tribe in which Gautama Buddha was a Prince. "Muni" means "One who teaches in silence," and there have been many such in India's long history. It must be remembered that the Buddha declared he had taught for forty-nine years but never uttered a word! This has deep meaning in an Absolute sense. So "Sakyamuni" is another name for the Buddha, the Perfect One.

SAMADHI — In traditional Indian meditation practice, as with Raja Yoga, Samadhi is the "super-conscious" state-without-thought that follows concentration and deep meditation. There are supposed to be two types of Samadhi, Nirvikalpa and Savakalpa, that with seeds and that in which all seeds (of Karma) have been burned and destroyed. Samadhi is the logical end of Indian practice, and that which is experienced in Samadhi is Truth. Yoga Vasistha, the teacher of Rama, spoke of entering the state of Samadhi for 100 years (a pre-determined time)! However, Buddhism uses the term differently. It means a constant sate of awareness, a twenty-four-hour enlightenment only possible to a realized Saint. Buddhism also speaks of certain types of Samadhi as they would of a particular practice, that is, the attaining of a particular type of consciousness.

SAMKHYA YOGA — The elaborate Samkhya Cosmology (and philosophy) is pretty well accepted by other beliefs in India. While Samkhya posits a limited dualism of non-sentient Nature (Prkrti) and the unchanging Reality (Purusha), the Yoga Philosophy of India has always accepted Samkhya as its base. There is a complete and wonderful account of the Samkhya beliefs in the long introduction to Mishra's *Textbook of Yoga Psychology.*

SAMSARA — The world of Maya, of Illusion. Where there is suffering, we are in Samsara, and this implies conditioned individual existence. When there is no longer such conditioned individual existence, there is no suffering, and we are then in our natural state, Nirvana. However, Zen makes much of the fact that "Samsara *is* Nirvana" — that is, right here in the suffering world we must find the perfection and the joy, not off in some transcendental place. This is quite different from the early Buddhism, where the idea was to "escape" from Samsara and enter Nirvana.

SAMSKARA — Literally means "Perfume." It refers to the tendency that may be left even after the habit-energy (vashana) has been destroyed. A heavy drinker might give up drinking (destroy the vashana), but there would always be the tendency to begin drinking again under the right conditions. This tendency lingers on as does the fragrance of perfume. Sometimes the word "samskara" is incorrectly used to designate the habit, which is really "vashana," the habit-energy.

SAMU — Refers to the absolute state of equality of Master and disciple in Zen practice (and when Zen people worked in the fields, giving rise to the saying, "A day without work is a day without food," which applied to the Master as well as the pupils). Zen has never made a differentiation between lay person and monk, either — all possess the Buddha Nature.

SAMURAI — During the Feudal days of Japan, the Samurai were the warrior class, lower than the Shogun or the Daimyo (Lords) but still noble and far above the farmer, artisan, business person, etc. Generally Samurai were "knights" in the service of some great Lord, to whom they owed their allegiance, but there were unattached Samurai known as "Ronin." Most Samurai lived by the Code of the Bushido, which was spelled out in the classic Hagakure. (See Tanaka and Stone's translation of the Hagakure known, in English, as "The Way of the Samurai.") Samurai can generally be recognized in pictures by the distinctive knotted headdress and by the two swords, one long and one short, that were usually carried.

SANSKRIT — The ancient language of India, often called "the Perfect Language." As the "Indo-European" language, it is sometimes felt to be the base for most modern European languages and of Latin and Greek as well. It is not spoken in India today, but it is the written language of scholarship, and along with Pali (which resembles Sanskrit), was the language of the original Buddhist Sutras (Scriptures).

SANZEN — In Rinzai Zen, the monk — or disciple — frequently enters the Master's chambers to give his or her view on one's Koan in the interview known as "the Kill-or-be-Killed" confrontation. This is Sanzen. There is usually a small ritual or ringing a bell, bowing, etc., that takes place before the aspirant enters and as he or she is leaving. It is only recently that a third person, an interpreter, has been allowed in Sanzen, in Japan, a practice much frowned upon by purists.

SATIPATTHANA — The great Meditation of "Mindfulness" spoken of in so many Sutras of the so-called Pali Canon. Usually the Buddha is believed to have said, "Here dwells the monk, mindful of —," and then follow the four categories of "Body — through the breath," "Feelings — before emotion," "State of Mind" and "Objects of Mind." These have innumerable sub-categories. It is actually one of the most complicated mental meditations devised by humans and, in the extreme, tends to break down all factors of consciousness. It is not to be practiced casually by the mildly-interested.

SATORI — From the Japanese verb "Satoru," meaning "to realize," this noun refers to the sudden experience often accompanied by profuse perspiration, of "The Great Joy." It is a profound enlightenment experience but not always final. Hakuin speaks of his original "incomplete" Satori, which brought on an arrogance that he later warned against, and of many "great" Satori experiences in addition to numerous "minor" Satoris. Soto Zen believes in letting the Satori experience come slowly, like ripening fruit, while Rinzai Zen tries to force the experience through intensive Koan study. Master Joshu Sasaki speaks of two types of Satori (Daigo and Saigo); the one in which complete unity is experienced, making it difficult for the one who experienced that unity to continue in his or her daily life, and the other in which one observes one's own Satori and then makes the complete circle, in which "mountains are again simply mountains," bringing one back into the activity of the world.

SECRET OF THE GOLDEN FLOWER — An esoteric book of Chinese Taoism, carefully worded so as to keep "inside" knowledge from the uninitiated. It instructs the reader in how to form an "immortal spirit body" within the perishable physical frame, dealing with alchemy in the purely spiritual sense. It is my opinion that present-day versions of this classic work contain many modern accretions. Very difficult reading without a background in Taoism.

SENGAI — An eighteenth century Japanese Zen Master known for his remarkable drawings in brush-and-ink.

SENSE BASES — In Buddhism, it is stressed that there are six sense bases, internal and external. The six bases, with their external fields are: Eye - Visible Forms; Ear - Sounds; Tongue - Flavor; Nose - Smells; Body - Tactual Objects; and Mind - Mind Objects. Note that "Mind" is considered a sense in this group.

SESSHIN — Any time a group of Zen adherents comes together for sitting meditation, it is "Sesshin." However, the term generally is used to describe a seven-day meditation session, in which the practitioners live at the temple or zendo (often without bathing and with very little sleep). This can be called a "Dai-Sesshin," generally translated as "Great- Sesshin," though Master Joshu Sasaki say it means "Sesshin-in-itself." At one period in Japan, the language took on frills and Sesshin was referred to as "O-Sesshin," the "O" being an honorific.

SESSHU — Often called "The Rembrandt of the Orient," Sesshu was, at one time, a Zen Buddhist monk who studied with Josetsu at Shokoko-ji (the Shokoko temple in Kyoto), Josetsu's student Shubun and, in China, with the Master Kakei (Hsin-Kuei in Chinese). Sesshu was a Master of every brush style and a great teacher as well. His most famous paintings, one of which was a series of panels depicting the change of the seasons, were done in what is called the "Suiboku" style.

SEVEN FACTORS OF ENLIGHTENMENT — These are: Mindfulness, Investigation of Reality, Energy, Rapture, Tranquility, Concentration, and Equanimity. These categories are associated with traditional Buddhism more than with modern Zen.

SHAOLIN(G) — Sometimes spelled with the "g," sometimes without, Shaolin(g) was the Chinese temple at which Bodhidharma, in the sixth century, sat facing the wall for nine years. It is also the temple at which he introduced "shadow-boxing," so Shaolin(g) is really the home of the Chinese Martial Arts.

SHEN-HSIU — Head monk and meditation Master at the temple of Hung-jen, the Fifth Zen (Ch'an) Patriarch when Hui-neng arrived there. Considerably older than Hui-neng (who was then 22), Shen-hsiu was passed over by the patriarch, who gave the robe and bowl to Hui-neng, making the latter the Sixth — and last — Patriarch. Shen-hsiu later had considerable success in founding his own school, which became known as "The Northern School" of Ch'an, teaching a type of concentrative meditation very much like Indian Dhyana, emphasizing purity. Later, Shen-hsiu was well established at the court of the emperor, to whom he specifically recommended Hui-neng as being the successor of the Fifth Patriarch. It was after Shen-hsiu's death that his school began to decline, and the Southern School (which taught "sudden enlightenment" and the Prajna Wisdom of one's own mind, in contradistinction to the quietism of the Northern School) became dominant, so much so that Shen-hsiu's teaching eventually disappeared.

SHIBUI — A noun in Japanese, but by adding the sound "no," it becomes an adjective describing a condition much like the difficult "Wabi Sabi" of the Japanese language. It implies an understatement, an austerity that does not necessarily mean poverty but an austere condition-by-choice, a naturalness and a lack of any flamboyance. The great Saigo, when he was "Prime Minister" of Japan, owned only one kimono and could not see visitors while it was being washed. As the kimono became worn and frayed, it probably also took on the "Shibui" characteristic much revered by Japanese. This was by Saigo's choice in much the same way that elaborate houses were sometimes describe by Lords as "My Hut." The Japanese do not respect overstatement, but they do venerate age. A four hundred-year-old door that had withstood many storms could well be described as "shibui," but not when it was new.

SHIKAN-TAZA — The word "Shika" implies "nothing but" in Japanese, and this may be what the "shikan" refers to, as Shikan-Taza is "nothing but Zazen" that is, no Koan or other device is used by the sitter, who simply stays for long periods of time in the meditation posture. The term is mostly used by Soto Zen in Japan.

SHIN BUDDHISM — All schools of the Amida Cult use the Nembutsu (Hail to the Buddha of Infinite Light — Namu Amida Butsu) and all belong to the classification "Shin" Buddhism.

SHINRAN — Founder of the great Jodo Shinshu Buddhist sect of Japan, part of the so-called "Amida Cult." Shinran appeared in the twelfth century (as did so many spiritual figures in the Far East). First a Tendai monk on the top of Mount Hiei (near Kyoto), Shinran later became the disciple of Honen, gave up his own efforts and surrendered to the Buddha of Infinite Light. When exiled from the Kansai area in Japan, he went to the distant islands and began a walking ministry, bringing this simple

"Other-Power" belief to the farmer and the other ordinary folk. Not a monk (he was married, which was frowned upon in those days), Shinran was also not a lay person. D.T. Suzuki has often written of him that he was the most appealing Christ-like religious figure in the Orient. His classic "Jodo Wasson" and other works are hard to find in English, but they are very popular in Japan.

SHOBOGENZO — Title of the great written work of Dogen Zenji, founder of Soto Zen in Japan. Not only is it considered "canon" by Soto Zennists, it is also recognized as one of the great philosophic works of Japan because of such provocative parts as the one on "Being-Time." Dogen wrote it in the popular Japanese language of the time, and it took twenty years to complete.

SHOKOKU-JI — One of the "Big Five" Rinzai Zen temples of Kyoto, this rather austere place is located near the emperor's palace and has played a big role in the development of Zen in Japan. I estimate that there are ten or eleven sub-temples on the broad Shokoku-ji grounds, and one of these is frequently used in the filming of Samurai movies.

SITAR — A large Indian instrument of the "guitar" family, still very popular in the music of India today. Ravi Shankar is a great instrumentalist of the sitar.

SITTING — Zen meditation of the sitting type is known as "Zazen" in Japan, and it is often referred to simply as sitting. Naturally, it implies cross-legged sitting in the meditation pose.

SIXTH PATRIARCH — Hui-neng became the Sixth Patriarch, succeeding Hung-jen, the Fifth Patriarch in the long line stretching back to Maha Kasyapa and the Buddha, 500 years before Christ. The Sixth Patriarch was also the last official patriarch in the numbered series. (The "Sixth" refers to the Chinese succession only, there supposedly having been a long line of 27 Indian patriarchs before Bodhidharma brought the succession and "transmission of mind" to China.)

SKANDHAS — Literally, "Heaps." These five constituents — Form (body), Feelings, Perceptions, Emotions and Consciousness — are, when joined together, the reason one believes there is a "person" or an entity. We are literally these "heaps." Buddhism denies any eternal Soul; consequently, when these five Skandhas disintegrate, where are "we"? This is a knotty question that many generations of Buddhists have pondered over. Notice that "Consciousness" is one of the ephemeral "heaps" in Buddhism, making it a "dharma" or non-lasting phenomenon. The very root of Buddhist belief and the basis of the non-Atman (An-Atman — no abiding Soul) declaration so revolutionary in India.

SOKA GAKKAI — Began in 1930 as a lay movement and revived in 1956. Toda Josei was the dynamic presence behind its growth to a size of over ten million members today. Claiming it is the fastest-growing religion in the world, Soka Gakkai first penetrated the Trade Unions and later became a powerful political force. The headquarters are in Taiseki-ji at the foot of Mount Fuji, and services are held there at midnight, complete with kettledrums. Soka Gakkai traces its tenets back to Nichiren, the great thirteenth century monk who was very intolerant of foreign influence; consequently, Soka Gakkai considers itself a Buddhist sect, though many Buddhist scholars dispute the idea. Fantastically organized, Soka Gakkai finds most of its teachings in "An Essay on Value," written by the founder, Makiguchi. There are three mystic Laws — that of the Gohonzon, which represents a "design" (Mandala) of the Universe and is to be worshipped; the Diamoku (or Invocation), serving somewhat the same purpose as the Nembutsu for Shin Buddhists, and the Kaidan or place of Instruction. As did Nichiren, the Soka Gakkai members look to the "Lotus Sutra" for truth and chant the "Namu Ryoho Renge Kyo" from that Sutra. Soka Gakkai has great Missionary spirit, and while it is separate from other Nichiren denominations in Japan, it is often known as "Nichiren Shoshu" in foreign lands.

SOTO ZEN — One of the three remaining Japanese Zen schools, it is the largest and has almost 15,000 temples. Dogen Zenji, the founder, brought some of the teachings of the Chinese Ts'ao Tung school back to Japan, and Soto is considered a Japanese continuation of Ts'ao Tung, though actually quite different.

SUCHNESS — In Sanskrit, "Tathata." It is my belief that the word "Tathagata" (a title for the Buddha, meaning "He who thus comes") originates from Tathata. There is no description for the Life Force or for the meaning of Life, and we can only refer to feelings too deep for words with the appellation, "suchness."

SUFI — Literally meaning "Cotton Clad," the Sufis are the Mystic Movement in Islam, though they claim they antedate Mohammed. The Dervishes are also Sufis, and poverty is looked upon as a "must" for members of this sect. The provocative Sufi teachings and sayings are beginning to reach the West in translation, but it is the Sufi Poets — such as Omar Khayam and Rumi — who are best known in the West. Many great Sufis were born in India, and it is felt that the great Sikh religion is an outgrowth of Sufi teaching.

SUIBOKU — There are many ways of using brush-and-ink in China and Japan (such as the "splashed-ink" style of some great Chinese artists). "Suiboku" is one of the styles, and it was greatly popularized by Sesshu and his disciples in Japan.

SUNYA — The doctrine of "emptiness" (Sunya) existed in India long before Gautama Buddha was born. This word for "Void," Sunya, occurs frequently in the Upanishads and in the Yoga Vasistha.

SUNYATA — The word Buddhists use to indicate the Void or "Emptiness," in contradistinction to "Sunya," which had been used in India before Buddhism. It is said that "Sunyata establishes all things without moving from Suchness."

SUTRAS — All Sutras (meaning "Scriptures") are supposedly the verbatim reports of the sermons of Gautama Buddha, beginning "Thus I have heard..." However, the sermons of Hui-neng, the Sixth Patriarch, are accorded the status of "Sutra" (Scriptural recognition), and we see the word Sutra used by such non-Buddhists as Patanjali in his "Yoga Sutras."

SUZUKI, D.T. — Suzuki Daisetz, who died recently, was a great Buddhist scholar and linguist. Once he held the chair in Indian Buddhism at Kyoto's Otani University, and another time he gave a long series of influential lectures, in English, at Columbia University in New York. Suzuki, who died in his mid-90s, greatly popularized Zen (particularly "Rinzai" Zen) in the West, but he himself was said to have been a Shin Buddhist all his life.

YUN-MEN — Known as "Ummon" in Japan. A brilliant Zen Master who died in the mid-tenth century, Yun-men was known for his "cakes," the sharp one-word answers he usually used. He was founder of one of the "Big Five" Chinese Ch'an schools.

For a complete catalog of other books & tapes by Justin F. Stone & additional authors, please contact:

Good Karma Publishing, Inc.
P.O. Box 511
Fort Yates, ND 58538
Telephone - 701/854-7459
Fax - 701/854-2004